Love Letters to My Girls

100+ Black Women Speak to the Hearts of Black Women & Girls

Love Letters to My Girls: *100+ Black Women Speak to the Hearts of Black Women & Girls*

Published in the United States by Spoonfed Motivation Publications.

ISBN 978-1-952870-00-2 (paperback)
ISBN 978-1-952870-01-9 (hardback)
Library of Congress Control Number: 2020910074

For permission, information requests, and bulk orders, write to the publisher at hello@spoonfedmotivation.com Subject: Spoonfed Motivation Publications.

Compiled by: Dr. Cherita Weatherspoon
Developmental Editors: Stephanie Lewis and Dr. Cherita Weatherspoon
Proofreader: Shelbie Myers
Cover Design: C.A. Canedo
Cover Art: Mari Dein
Interior Design: Amit Dey

"We are born authentic, creative, powerful and beautiful beings who are taught, or rather, forced, to conform—to transform even, to fit the small minds of those who fear us. Those who wish to be like us, to be us; those who recognize who we are. Then we must fight to be our true, powerful selves again. We fight against the lies we've been told and learned to believe. We fight against the images that tell us we are ugly and unacceptable. We fight against each other as if we cannot co-exist as sisters; as if there is not enough air for all of us to breathe. We fight against ourselves, legitimizing the lies, accepting the abuse, cowering down, hiding our hearts, holding back our power, silencing our voices. Sister; be you. Be all of you. You are magnificent. And you deserve to be a Black woman in this world."

—Dr. Cherita Weatherspoon

Dedication

Emile; my industrious, loyal, wise and loving
queen of a daughter—
this book is dedicated to you.
May you see the world through eyes of possibility
and see yourself as the wonderful creation you are.
You are loved more than you know.

Table of Contents

Acknowledgments

I celebrate, honor, and give thanks to the many supporters of this project. To the Black women and girls who saw the vision, helped to write it and bring it to pass; you are loved, and you are appreciated. Our legacies are now intertwined. May your voice live on as long as this world remains. Thank you!

To Stephanie Lewis: thank you for assisting me behind the scenes and helping to bring these words to life, so they might give life to our sisters who need it most.

To our sponsors and partners: thank you for believing in this work, and the potential of its impact on Black women and girls around the world. Your support will help spread this message far and wide.

To our donors: those who gave from their pockets to ensure that the most vulnerable of our sisterhood could benefit from this work. Thank you, thank you, thank you!

To our sisters: thank you for picking up this book, thank you for reading it, thank you for feeling it, thank you for letting it fuel you, thank you for being a light in this world. Thank you for being you. You, Black woman, are our inspiration.

To my family: thank you for tolerating late dinners, the laptop in the bed, my late nights in the office, and my ear-bending rants and musings. I could not do what I do, nor be who I am, without your love and support.

To my God: thank you for choosing me and for continuing to call me even when I didn't answer.

Preface

Emile was about eight at the time. I looked at her. I saw her. I pictured her as a Black woman—a Black woman in this world. There were so many lessons I wanted to teach her, to help prepare her. A Black woman in this world. I decided I would write her letters. Letters that would remind her of how beautiful she is, even when the world says otherwise. Letters that would encourage her when she felt defeated and wanted to give up. Letters that would inspire her to live the life she desires. Letters that would empower her to show up in the world authentically, knowing that she—as she is—is all she needs to be. Letters whose words would overpower and drown out the negativity and destructiveness of the lies she would hear repeatedly throughout her life about who she is, and who she is not. A Black woman in this world.

I never wrote those letters. I did, however, try to *live* those letters.

Now, fourteen years later, something stirs in my heart and I am moved to share those letters; those inspiring, uplifting, motivating and empowering words—not only with my daughter, but with daughters, mothers, sisters, aunties, friends—my sisters, around the world. Black women in this world.

But my story is only one story. My experience is only one experience. My voice is but one voice. So, I called. I called out to Black women in this world to join me in inciting a revolution of sisterhood. I called out to my sisters to join me in edifying and building up our Black women and girls. I called out to my sisters to give back, help out, and push up the women and girls in our communities; to remind them—and the world—how powerful we are. I called out to my sisters to help me inspire our sisters to embrace their uniqueness, power, intelligence, and beauty in order to change their mindsets so they can change themselves, then change the world.

My sisters—Black women and girls—answered the call. These letters are their response. These letters represent how they exist—how they have come to exist—as Black women in this world.

Introduction

Why This Book is Necessary

Quanisha Green, MSS and Cherita Weatherspoon, Ed. D

Black Women. Black Girls. Black Bodies. The criticism we hear and see e-ve-ry day of our lives feels like an erasure and devaluing of our communities, our cultures, our selves—the things we identify with and love the most.

We are ostracized and illegalized for the characteristics and traits with which we are born.

It's as if we were born a mistake.

A sin. An aberration. Even an abomination.

That is how we are made to feel.

By those in authority. By those who have no authority.

By those who have, and those who have not.

By those who lack this beautiful melanin and those who have it but somehow, for some reason, see themselves as different—not *really* Black.

We experience it from those who don't know better. From those who do, but don't care. From those who should know better.

From teachers.

From supervisors.

From peers.

From activists.

From social justice institutions.

We experience this.

On our jobs.

In our communities.

In our denominations.

In healthcare facilities.

We experience this.

At the grocery store.

Walking down the street.

Hailing a cab.

Covertly.

Overtly.

We experience this.

Through racism.

Through bias.

Through stereotyping.

Through intolerance.

Through exclusivity.

In hiring.

In firing.

We. Experience. This.

Yet, this is not who we are.

This is our experience.

- Little Black girls are sent home from school because their skirts, pants or dresses are too short or too tight because they may have thicker thighs or larger derrieres; their hair is seen as unkempt and not aligned with the dress code.
- Little Black girls are assaulted and raped because of their very existence; because the sway of their hips and the movement to their native instruments are interpreted as savage, animalistic, and hypersexual.
- Little Black girls are not viewed as children or granted the patience, kindness, and protection we extend to other children—those we *see* as children.
- Little Black girls are told their hair, bodies, and features are ugly, demonic, or animal-like. Images of beauty don't reflect what they see in a mirror, so they try to assimilate.
- Little Black girls grow up to be women who are overlooked for promotions and adequate compensation.
- Black Women are told they don't quite fit into the company culture.
- Black Women are identified as negating the feminist movement because they prioritize their racial/ethnic identity before their gender identity.
- Black Women can't express an educated opinion or make a statement of truth or fact without being labeled "aggressive" or "angry."

- Black Women can't ask for what they deserve from organizations, institutions, or men, without being viewed as "ungrateful."
- Black Women are hated because of their look, style and natural physical attributes, but those same attributes are loved on lighter, whiter skin—even when it's unnatural and fake.
- Black Women are not allowed to be women.
- Black Women are not allowed to BE.

This is our experience.

So yes, we need this book. WE BLACK WOMEN and GIRLS need this book. YOU, who are not Black women and girls, need this book.

We Black Women and Girls need to know how valuable we are.

How beautiful we are.

How powerful we are.

How intelligent we are.

How brilliant we are.

How loved we are.

How loveable we are.

How valid we are.

How worthy we are.

How strong we are.

How resilient we are.

How vulnerable we are.

How necessary we are.

How WE really ARE.

It's time WE, BLACK WOMEN and GIRLS, realize that.

It's time YOU—all of YOU, recognize the TRUTH.

Section One

YOU ARE...

...Worthy

To the Girl Unaware of Her Worth,

I have been you. I have walked in your shoes. I have seen through your eyes. Forgive me, but your eyes can be foolish at times. They might try to see things through a lens in which they were taught, rather than through the lens of truth. Truth is, you are worthy. Despite your flaws, you are worthy. Regardless of your grades, you are worthy.

Worth is not determined by *what* you are. It is determined by *who* you are, and *who* you are cannot be weighed, measured or graded. You see, there are concepts the camera cannot capture. There are grains of grace that cannot be grasped. What we can see is less than half of what there is.

It is unfortunate that we live in a world that profits from pain; a world that derives dollars from detrimental thoughts. We are constantly being told that we are not enough, that something is missing. When we think something is missing, we often go in search of it in peculiar places. Sometimes we search online, or in stores. Some (including myself) have even searched for whatever it may be in other people. This is not okay; normal, but not okay.

Everything you desire, everything you are searching for lives within you. The search is over. You are your other half, your own soulmate. You are the answer. I did not come to this realization until I was 16; that all the love I had been in search of existed within me. It is pretty crazy when you think about it. We've got all these bright, shiny things living in the external world, distracting us from our internal light. That's what I meant when I said your eyes can be foolish. They can be deceiving. Sometimes we only see what we are taught to see. Most of us are taught to see what society wants us to see. I refuse to be blinded by their vision of me.

Loving yourself has become an act of rebellion. I want to encourage each and every one of you to rebel with me; love yourself. Be true to you, because despite the pain, there is potential. There is hope. You will spend the rest of your life within yourself. Why not make it a nice place to be? Now, know your worth—then, add tax.

With love and light,

Essynce Moore

Sister-Friend,

Let me tell you something. You are worthy. You have desirable qualities that are well overdue for the respect you may not have received.

You are worthy of love. A love that is true and healthy. A love that is honest and noble. A love that you never thought was possible for you. This love can come in any form. Whether it be a boyfriend turned husband, a friend turned family, or a twinkle in God's eye turned into a child. This love will have hardships, but the love you have will be what gets you through.

You are worthy of peace. A peace that will consume all aspects of life. This is a peace that you'll find within yourself. It's where you'll go at your worst moments, in your darkest times. It will give you the space and tranquility you need to process, compose, plan, and execute the problem and solution.

You are worthy of stability. I know life is a rollercoaster, and it will throw you a few curveballs, but there will be a stable aspect in your life. Find a person you love and trust, an activity you love, and spiritual guidance. These three things should be the most consistent things in your life. They will give you a routine you can run with and plan around in the craziest of seasons.

You are worthy of self-love. The love you should have for yourself is the greatest love you will ever have. So, you need to make sure it is the best you can imagine. You do not need a man to live for, or to love yourself.

Look at yourself. What do you see? I see a beautiful Black woman. I see a loving, honest, industrious, respectful, helping, humble, empathetic and confident woman. I want you to find a quote, phrase or verse to recite every day about yourself. Or you can use mine: "You are beautiful. You are strong. You are smart—ten times smarter than the rest. You work hard. You work smart. You are loved. You are independent.

You are compassionate. You can do all things through Christ, who strengthens you! You will have an amazing day, Love."

You are worthy of friendship. You need not isolate yourself. You deserve to have friends. Real friends. True friends. The kind you can trust with your life; who respect and honor you. The friends you call your brothers and sisters. They should be the ones you go to in good times and bad. They would be *your person.* For me, they are the people I would trust my future children's lives with if I were no longer to live on earth.

Sister, beautiful Black queen, you are worthy of every good, amazing and right thing on this earth. I pray that you shall receive it in all of its abundance.

Peace, love, joy and blessings!

Emile Weatherspoon

Dear Sister,

I remember those talks with my mom as she drove me to school. Each day before I exited the car, the school bell ringing in the background and kids scrambling to get in line, she would grab my arm, look me in the eye, and say, "Remember, you are fearfully and wonderfully made." Not realizing the importance of what she was saying, I would gather my belongings, scurry out of the car, and give my mom a quick, "OK! Love you."

At the time, I had no idea that she was speaking Psalm 139:19 into my life. "I will praise You, for I am fearfully and wonderfully made; Marvelous are Your works" (NKJV). She was telling me I was worthy because she knew a day would come when I didn't feel as if I were. She also knew she would not always be around to remind me. Like most of us, I doubted my ability. Many times, I took the low road to show I was a team player because they said it wasn't my time to shine. You probably know what I'm talking about, because you've probably been delayed and denied, too.

At some point, like me, you'll reach a moment in your life when you are tired of giving in and having your voice silenced. You may want to have someone you love (and who loves you) remind you just how wonderful you are and push you to speak up and show up. But what do you do when no one is there? Who will remind you how valuable you are in your loneliest and darkest times?

I leaned on the words that my mother spoke to me so many times. As I dug deeper into that verse and studied it, reading it in different translations and meditating on its meaning, it literally blew my mind. Those words now serve as a constant reminder that I was created by God with a purpose! I hope these words speak to you, "You made all the delicate, inner parts of my body and knit me together in my mother's womb. Thank you for making me so wonderfully complex! Your workmanship is marvelous—how well I know it" (Psalm 139:13-14 NLT).

These words allow me to walk in boldness, because they remind me daily that I am worthy. You should know that you are worthy. You were custom created, knitted together with purpose and intention. Every unique detail of your being was hand-picked and added to your design. How worthy and valuable you are!

What other people said you can't accomplish? Now is the time to show them it can be done. That idea they said wouldn't work? Now is the time to show them how it works. That seat at the table you've been trying to get? Pull up your own chair. Better yet, bring your own table! The point is, you can have whatever you desire, because your desires were placed in you by your Creator, and your Creator made you worthy!

Love,

Marcie Wilson

Dear Sister,

Throughout your life you will encounter many people and situations. Sometimes those people don't have good intentions, and sometimes those situations will cause you to make decisions that might not be in your best interest. No decision you make (no matter how bad) will ever lessen your worth. Your worth cannot be destroyed. Some things are out of your control and others are in your control, but life is about making mistakes, and experiencing things you'd never thought you'd experience.

You might feel you're less of a person because of something you've done, or something that has happened to you. You might feel less beautiful, less special, less amazing, less worthy. I'm here to tell you, you are worthy. I wish someone would have told me when I was a little younger that it was okay to make mistakes; that it wasn't the end of the world if I messed up. We can always learn from our mistakes, but our mistakes don't determine who we are. Our mistakes don't diminish our worth. It is important to value yourself, so you'll never settle for less than you deserve. Value yourself because you are priceless. You are beautiful. You can do anything you set your mind to. You will be successful, and all good things will come your way as long as you keep pressing. You are loved, and you are precious. If no one else has told you, let me tell you: no matter what happens in your life, you will always be worthy.

You might have heard of that motivational speech where they take a dollar bill, crumble it up, step on it, and rip it to prove that no matter what it has been through, it still keeps its value. Obviously, you are worth more than a dollar, but the message is so powerful. Life is going to take you through ups and downs, and at times it will feel like your life is filled with nothing but downs. The downs can really take a toll on you. My downs would really stress me out to where I was diagnosed with depression and anxiety. It is normal to be overwhelmed by your downs, but it is important to remember that for every down, there is an up on its way. The best way to enjoy your ups and remain mentally healthy is to remember that your downs do not define you, and do not make you any less worthy of your ups.

The color of your skin does not diminish your worth. The color of your skin makes your outside as beautiful as your inside. You are worthy! Your mental health does not diminish your worth. It is okay to not be okay. Find someone to confide in; it's not a bad thing to ask for help. You are amazing, and you are worthy! Not having expensive clothes and materialistic things does not diminish your worth. Your neighborhood does not diminish your worth. Your school does not diminish your worth. Your family situation does not diminish your worth. Your popularity, the number of friends you have, your relationship status—none of that diminishes your worth. Your worth will never be depleted. You were created because you have a unique purpose in life. You don't have to know what your purpose is right now; just know that your life is purposeful, and everything happens for a reason. Never settle, and never second guess yourself, because you are and always will be worthy!

Your friend,

Tina Natasha

To the Beautiful Black Queen Searching for Worthiness,

There is a misconception that we have to have someone else to be strong—whether it be a man, woman, mother, father, sister, or brother. All that we need is right inside of us. A light is there waiting to be released. It is waiting for the chance to shine and be seen, but it's being hidden, and dampened by feelings of unworthiness and fear. I understand this, and so many of us have been there. So, know that you are not alone.

I remember hitting a moment of vulnerability and entering an emotional space I thought I would never experience. In that vulnerable space I experienced hurt, criticism, and second-guessed my self-worth. I felt unworthy of being a woman. Queen, I know what it's like to be a strong, confident, and dynamic woman one day, then experiencing something that makes you feel worthless the next day.

I also know the struggle to find that one reason that will bring you out of the dark and back to that confident, strong, dynamic, worthy woman. I urge you to find your "why," search for your passion, and dig deep into the one thing that makes each day worth living in your truth unapologetically. Live your life boldly, fearlessly, and authentically while soaring to what's next for you—never settling for the comfort of right now. Because Queen, you are worth so much more. If you've never heard this before, and it's never left the lips of someone who cares: you are worthy.

I, along with so many other women, care and want you to know that we support you. We are rooting for your success in all that you want to do in life. If you don't know what success looks like for you and you are still doubting your worthiness, I want you to make a bold decision today. Decide to give yourself a chance. Now breathe, and fully realize that you have something worth sharing. Take a deep breath in right now. Now exhale. Say out loud, "I am worthy. I am enough."

Just in case you still don't believe it, choose to show yourself compassion. Let compassion wrap its arms around you and engulf you, allowing you to accept the truth of your worthiness, despite your imperfections, mistakes, and failures. We all need compassion, and when we can't get it from others, we need to know how to give it to ourselves. We need to know that it's okay to make mistakes. We can be wrong, and if we fail, it does not mean we are weak. It simply means we are human.

I want to lend you some of the compassion I hold in my heart for you, hoping you will use it to amplify the compassion for yourself that may be buried deep inside. Let it explode into your heart, mind, soul and body. Allow it to show up and show out for you. In that moment, accept yourself, accept your truth, and share your amazingness with the world. I urge you to become the leader of your own life and take charge of the direction you are headed. No one has a right to tell you what that is. You don't have the right to not accept your purpose and deny the world of everything that it was meant to be given through you, because you don't believe you are worthy. You are here for a reason. You are nothing less than amazing. You are strong. You are worthy.

With love,

Cameasha Muhammad

My Dear Beautiful Black Sister,

I hope this letter finds you in the highest of spirits and excitement! I'm incredibly happy to be in touch with you. I've been thinking about what to say and what comes to mind, sis, are my conversations with God. I'm just going to share what's on my heart. I think that will be a good start. Recognizing and saying what's on your heart is not always easy; however, it's a cleansing of the soul that becomes easier the more you do it. Really! And, of course, it matters who you say it to. I'm choosing to share my heart with you.

First, a lesson on life. Did you know that the universe and life are two of your best friends? When you give the universe your innermost desires and goals, it will deliver life (the irreplaceable teacher) to you on a silver platter. Be ready, sis. You deserve for your outrageous dreams to come true, to be happy, to have joy and even to experience pain. You are strong enough to stand up to and face pain and then reap the rewards that come on the other side. I am so proud of you for that! Be grateful for those lessons. Be willing to put in the work for the life you desire. You hold the key to your happiness, growth and confidence.

A lesson on happiness. Between you and I, sis, I was furious with my husband when he told me I expected him to make me happy and that I needed to do that for myself. I thought, "Well, what do I need you for then?" As much as it hurt to hear his words, I realized it was true. His words made me recognize that I didn't like how I felt but that I deserved to be happy, so I searched for happiness in and through myself. Know that you deserve happiness and know that you are responsible for your own happiness. Life will allow you to experience pain even when you don't deserve it, but it will also bring you joy and happiness. It's up to you to experience it when it's there. That's what I prayed for. The universe responded to me with that silver platter. You are a beautiful, loving Black woman and you deserve happiness. Find it wherever you can and create it wherever it is lost.

Now, a lesson on loving yourself. I'm open to hearing and learning from the universe and life wherever those lessons might come from. Music is often one of those sources. A line from "I Remember" by Keyshia Cole hit my heart and spoke to me in a way that reminded me to love myself while also loving others: "For the rest of my life, I promise myself I would love me first genuinely."

I say to you my beautiful Black sister, be proud of your Blackness and your womanhood. Live and experience life to the fullest. Create your own happiness and joy in the world. Love yourself fully and out loud. Never be ashamed of who you are. Be strong and confident. Own your worthiness. Life is waiting for you. Hold your head up high and be proud. Accept nothing less than the respect you deserve, in the way you feel respected.

I love you Sis,

Gwen Buchanan

...Valuable

Hello Sweetheart,

I love you. You mean the world to me. It doesn't matter if you're struggling to find your way and grappling with new experiences, or if life is one big party and you're breezing along. I believe in you and support you. Know that you'll make mistakes along the way. Accept that you'll also experience and accomplish great things. Never be afraid to step out of your comfort zone. Seize life as it comes. Become a lifelong learner. Whatever road you travel—it's important that you first learn to be a healthy, happy, single woman before becoming the wife, mother and/or professional you were meant to become. Learning to love yourself and being comfortable in your own skin is the foundation of success! Yes, you can succeed without self-love, but you'll be miserable.

As a 63-year-old, never-married, childless woman, I discovered that I had the gift of singleness in my 30's. Although it's been quite a journey, I have no regrets and wouldn't change my life for anything! Whatever your path, follow it passionately, and live life to the fullest so you too will have no regrets. While not everyone chooses a life of singleness, everyone navigates life as a single person. We're born individually, and ultimately will die alone. It doesn't matter if you come from a large family, have tons of friends, are married, in a relationship, or attend lots of social events.

Have you ever felt alone, even when surrounded by others? We all have. It's okay to be alone. Being consumed by loneliness, however, is a different story. That's why self-love is crucial. I'm a firm believer in the power of affirmations. Learning to appreciate your strength and value as a single woman will enhance every area of your life. To help you appreciate your worth, I've created an acronym for *valuable,* and want you to embrace and memorize it.

I am:

Victorious. The mere fact that I was born makes me victorious. I was destined to be here, to occupy space, thrive, and succeed!

Astounding. My presence and impact on others and the world will be astounding!

Laudable. I will live my life so that I am deserving of praise and accolades, but I don't need them to know my value.

Unique. There is not—nor will there ever be—anyone else like me on this planet!

Ambitious. I will always keep a dream in my heart and strive to achieve it!

Beautiful. I will cultivate my inner beauty, which will enhance my outer beauty!

Lovable. I am worthy of love and will share my love with those who know how to love me!

Exquisite. The essence and energy of my light will shine so bright that it leaves an unmistakable impression on others!

Regardless of what anyone says, does or believes, you are valuable. Own it, claim it, and wear it proudly wherever you go!

Love,

LaVerne Henderson

Dear Beautiful Queens and Daughters,

Remember these words: You are valuable. I am writing this letter to let you know how valuable you are to me. When I think about value, it reminds me of a diamond. A diamond has to go through a process, and in the end will shine despite its transitions. It goes through a melting process, then is formed into different shapes and sizes. No matter the size of the diamond—it still has significant value, just like you. Whether you are short, tall, curvy, slim, rocking your natural curls or long-weaved hair; whether your skin is chocolate or caramel brown, your uniqueness and beauty shine bright.

I wonder, what do you see when you look in the mirror? When I look at you, I see a beautiful Black queen who was created with greatness for this earth. I see a woman who can speak with power and strength. I see a girl who recognizes that her trials, tribulations, and truths will make her stronger and wiser. I see a sister who walks in the room with boldness and knows her worth. I see a queen who can recognize and honor other queens.

I pray that you see yourself as I see you, and that you will not let your fears block your destiny. I hope you'll learn to admit when you are wrong and show grace to others when they have wronged you. I hope you'll use your words to affirm yourself and others. I pray that you will use the power within you to change the world for the better. I wonder if your past will push you forward, or if you will allow it to pull you back. I wonder if you will give up—but then I remember; you are a queen. A queen knows her worth. As long as you recognize yourself as the queen you are, I know you will be okay. I know you will move beyond surviving and you will thrive.

Lastly, my beautiful queen, don't wait for someone else to tell you how precious you are. You must know your worth even when others around you don't. There will be days when you are alone and have to enjoy and be content with who you are;

however, you must know who you are. I dare you to look yourself in the mirror every day, speak your name, and tell yourself you are valuable: Victorious, Ambitious, Loyal, Unique, Amazing, Beautiful, Loved, Elegant. Words are powerful and have the ability to build you up or tear you down. Let these words empower and strengthen you. You are valuable.

Love,

Brenda Searcy

Dear Daughter,

I thought I would have more time to guide you as you grew, and yet there are still so many topics we are supposed to discuss in more depth. I still have the list: God and Faith, Sisterhood, Peer Pressure, Courage, Body Image and Self Esteem, Sexuality and Boys, Drugs and Alcohol, Honesty and Integrity, Seasons, and Personal Safety and Hygiene.

And now, time has slipped away so fast, and you are all grown up. But I want to tell you something before you go off on your own: you have been and will always be enough.

You are enough.

Your hair may be long, or short, it might lay down, or stand up in protest. It may be brown, black, or different shades of the rainbow, but it is your crown. Wear it proudly. Your hair, in all of its majestic glory, is enough.

You are enough.

Your skin may have pimples, it may be smooth and well-moisturized, it may be dry with wrinkles, or have tiny freckles and one or two moles. But remember, skin only goes so deep, and what you invest and deposit on the inside will manifest on the outside. So, take care to feed your soul with plenty of laughter and kindness, and your skin will be a shield of armor to protect you. Your body is enough.

You are enough.

Your thighs may be thick and your hips wide, or your thighs skinny and your hips narrow. You may birth a nation through the parting of your thighs and the widening of your hips, or from the stroke of your pen or keyboard, or from your resounding voice as the next great orator. The choice remains yours. Your choices are enough.

You are enough.

Give unconditionally to those who are in need and know that a philanthropic heart is one that is close to God. When your energy, patience and good spirits run low, remember to stop and replenish yourself, and know that it's okay to take time for you. Your "no" is enough.

You are enough.

People will always talk about you, against you, for you, with you in good and bad ways; let them because from your head down to your toes—from a time before you were conceived—you have been and will always be enough.

Love,

Dalila Zachary

To My Beautiful Sisters,

I'm writing to let you know that I value you. I value you, because I am you. People value different things. Some value material things, or fame and fortune, and for others, it's family, or God. You are valuable because God created you. You are precious and priceless. Your job is to shine and let the world know your value.

You are beautiful, gifted and creative. Take the time to discover who you are, and then walk confidently in that. You have what it takes to do or be whatever you want. I want you to accept yourself for who you are; tall, short, round, thin, short haired or long haired—who cares! You have to love yourself more each day. You have to commit to pleasing your Creator and yourself—not people. People—whether family, friends or employers—will try to define who you are or put a label on you. Knowing who you are is your power.

So what, you were born on the wrong side of the tracks? So what, your father wasn't in your life? So what, you were molested? You were still created with value. This may not be your story; you may have had it all, and still felt worthless. I'm here to let you know, you are beautiful. Cry if you need to but keep smiling. Don't stay in that place. Use your power to pull yourself up. Sometimes the pressure you are under is there to produce the diamond in you.

Because you are a diamond, people will be attracted to your shine. You must be careful who you allow in your space. Friends encourage you and are supportive. They will also tell you when you are wrong or could do better. Friends don't make you feel or look bad to make themselves look better. Friends respect who you are and what you believe. So, if you have one or two good friends, value them.

Value your thoughts. What you think about yourself and the world around you is what you will create. It is the same with what you say. Your words will create your experience. Don't be afraid of failure; try. There is a valuable lesson in trying even if you fail. Let others know how to treat you. Never be afraid to speak up for what you believe. Never depend on others to affirm you. Look in the mirror every day and affirm yourself. The next time someone says what's up, confidently reply "My value!"

You got this girl!

Cheering for you,

Lisa Michelle Flynn

Dear Beautiful Black Girl,

Chin up. Stand tall. Drop your shoulders. You will change the world by simply being you.

I remember one of my lowest moments; I felt alone, unloved, and undeserving. I placed my value in the hands of others because I didn't believe in myself. I remember how difficult it was for me to believe in something I didn't see, even though it was something I always felt. I had to refocus, reset and remember that my worth was determined by me. I had to make a decision at that moment, that this was not going to be my life. If only I had known then what I know now. That all the moments of confusion, unhappiness, and uncertainty were preparing me for amazing things ahead.

I am able. I am deserving. I am loved. I am valuable.

Sweet girl, if I could teach you anything in this world, it would be that you can rise from anything. You can completely recreate yourself at any given moment. There will be moments where you doubt yourself, and that is normal. In these moments you have to show up for yourself. You have built a foundation of self-assurance strong enough that nothing and no one will ever make you question your value. There will be times when your faith will be tested, and you'll need to walk by sight. In these times, you'll be required to show up for yourself like never before.

You will be presented with lessons over and over until you learn the lesson. You hold the power to live the life of your dreams. Not the life that looks good, but the life that feels good. You are worthy of placing yourself in places that add to your life, not take away. In a world where there are so many liabilities, you, baby girl, are an asset. You add value to everything you'll ever touch. Don't subject yourself to anything or anyone that devalues you and all you stand for, because that kind of person ain't your person. You take ordinary things and make them extraordinary. For that, you have to be protective of who you allow into your sacred space.

You are a diamond. You are a star. You are phenomenal. You are loved. You are appreciated. You are valuable. Please, don't ever forget it.

Loving you as you grow into the beautiful woman you are destined to be,

Petra Sherbin-Fox

To My Priceless Jewels,

Do you know your value? Some of us don't know our value; some of us know our value but misuse it; and some of us know our value, but let others abuse it. This letter is for my girls who know their value but use it to manipulate or allow themselves to be manipulated. I know you're wondering where I am going with this.

Value is represented in how you behave, your standards, and what is important to you. Let's think about that. How we behave, our principles and judgment are examples of how valuable we believe we are. With that in mind, what do your regular practices and conduct say about your self-worth?

The world sees women largely as objects and sexual beings. This has been demonstrated in images of women since the beginning of time. Think about how female cartoons and dolls are depicted. They are usually well-endowed, embellished and highlighted in a way that makes them attractive to their male counterparts. Fast-forward to today, and we see how women are depicted in social media, TV, movies, magazines and commercial products. Let's face it; sex sells, but that should not dictate how we value ourselves. We are more than sexual beings to be used to pleasure men. We are just as important, intelligent, and capable as any man.

I want to encourage you to stand your ground, keep your value, and never compromise. You may be in a relationship or have friends who pressure you to have sex. You are valuable; you can say no! You may find yourself in a situation where you believe you need to sell your body, expose it, or strip to earn money. You are valuable; you can say no! There will be times you feel lonely, alone, or lost and it may seem like sex will heal those woes—it won't. You can say no! Using your body as a resource may appear to be the best or easiest option to resolve feelings of inadequacy, your desire to be loved, or get what you want. I've been there and I know that sex is never the answer. Your body was never meant to be used that way. I want to be clear that sex is not a bad thing and having sex does not mean you don't value yourself; that is not what I'm saying. What I am saying is to preserve the beauty and value of your body and the gift of sex for your loving and worthy partner who will honor you in a way you deserve.

I hope this letter causes you to reflect on how you are loving and honoring yourself in body, mind, and spirit and inspires you to see yourself as a precious jewel. Using your body or sex for gain is a gross misuse of your temple. It also puts you at risk for disease, unplanned pregnancy, and establishes soul ties to people you may not want to be connected to for life. Yes, it really is that deep. Sex is that deep.

As a Black woman, you are absolutely sexy. Being sexy however, doesn't mean you have to give your body away and allow it to be used, abused and discarded as if it has no value. You are priceless. Make sure the person you decide to share yourself with recognizes and honors that. You must recognize and honor it as well.

With Love,

Tanerra Willis

Dear Black Queen,

Are you ready for a lesson? Black Queen, you may not have been taught just how wonderful God made you. Yes, you are fearfully and wonderfully made. Black Queen, you are wise, and everything that your heart desires you are capable of achieving, and more.

At one time in my life, I didn't realize my worth. Have you ever been in that position? The first time I recall feeling inferior was in the 4th grade. My teacher held me back from the 5th grade because of a standardized test score. Having to repeat 4th grade made me think I was dumb. That was a lie. After that experience, my grades improved, and I performed better on standardized tests. In middle school, I made the honor roll and was happy to see progress. That progress came with being ridiculed and called a white girl. Let's set the record straight. Black Queen, when you are performing at your best, you are not "acting white." You are presenting your best self to the world.

For many Black Queens, these feelings of inadequacy from childhood continue into adulthood. As a result, you treat yourself poorly, and because you don't realize your worth, you believe you need to work yourself to death to attain greatness. Whether it's a degree or job promotion, you have conditioned yourself to go above and beyond to the extreme—even to your detriment. Whatever God desires for your life will manifest in His time. Yes, there will be work involved, but it won't include self-neglect. That's where we mess up. The first thing we give up or delay in pursuit of our goals is caring for ourselves. Unfortunately, years of neglect will wreak havoc on your body. Ask me how I know.

Black Queen, you are magnificent and deserve greatness. In every aspect of your life you should give yourself the best. Feed yourself real food and avoid junk. Your body is a temple that deserves to be honored and taken care of. You would never visit a mansion and toss trash around the property. You understand the mansion is beautiful and want to do your part to keep it that way. Think the same way about your body. You are vivacious and divine, worth far too much to deface with garbage.

Surround yourself with people who celebrate you and what you bring to the world and not just tolerate you. When you are around people who connect with the real you, your mindset will change. These people will support your dreams and help you discover how capable and powerful you are.

Can I share something with you, Black Queen? I don't want it to take you the amount of years it took me to realize my value and stop neglecting myself. I want you to come to that realization today. You are priceless! No one and no experience can take away your worth. No matter what this life brings, always believe in yourself and your value.

Love,

Cassandra Hill

Dear Black Mothers, Black Daughters, and Black Sisters,

I am writing to tell you how much I love you, and how each of your lives, at this very moment, are inspiring every part of my soul! Your lives are a demonstration of what endurance, fighting, and strength look like! Through it all, here you are today, still covered in the beauty of who you truly are! You are still here, still standing. Somewhere down on the inside of you is a river stirring deep that must be inspired to rise. I honor you today with words of love; may my words lift your heart, empower your soul, and encourage your day.

As I looked in the mirror this morning, I saw the reflection of your pain and your grief looking back at me. I must tell you; I recognized the pain and grief I saw. There is no doubt most of us were born into "circumstances." Circumstances that tried to shape you, break you and make you into something other than who you were created to be. I want to remind you that the senseless trauma you experienced and the evils you endured do not define you! Please hear the heart of your sister calling out to you to rise from the ashes of your pain right now! Rise out of the pain of your sorrows! Rise and speak to it and tell it, "No more will you rule and rob from me!"

I am one of many of your sisters calling out to you because your life carries so much value, and someone is waiting to hear your voice, see your strength, and experience your power! Success is calling your name, and the dreams inside your heart must be set free. The dreams you carry must be born; they must come forth. The dreams you carry are filled with life and liberty for those you are called to touch. Black mothers, Black daughters, Black sisters; I want to ask something important of you today. Would you go to your mirror and look closely at the beautiful reflection looking back at you? What do you see? Let me tell you what I see. I see your smiles that light the room, your unaged skin, and the sparkle in your eyes telling your story. I see the magnificence of your power, your uniqueness and your exquisite love, and it is beautiful! Did you see what I just saw? Hey, you must see that you are beautiful inside and out! Your power is seen when you love, give, and nurture. It is love that motivates you to extend your heart and your hands. That beautiful love that comes from deep inside you can never be taken away. The powerful love that motivates you to keep embracing, keep enduring, keep living—that is what I saw, and that is what others see; your beautiful love, and your great power.

Black mothers, Black daughters, Black sisters—speak to yourselves! Call out your name and say: "I am beautiful! I am powerful! I am love!" May your hearts continue to be filled with beautiful, powerful love, and may you be faithful to loving yourself. Let your beautiful Black voices be heard! Sing your songs, dream your dreams, and together let's change the world! Let us add the beauty and power we possess to this world to make it a better place for our Black daughters, our Black sisters, and our Black mothers to live, to love, and to rise!

With all my love,

jSelene Thornton-Hubbard

...Brilliant

Dear Sister,

The word *brilliant* is a positive term often used to describe the visual impression of a star, a diamond cut with precision, or an unusually clever individual. However, it is rarely used as a term to describe our astute Black girls. As a matter of fact, those with intellectual prowess are often categorized with derogatory names as "difficult," "misfits," or "rebels" instead. I believe that this results from the fear of our potential. Brilliant Black girls and women are phenomenal!

For hundreds of years, our beauty and sensuality have been marketed while our brilliance has been dimmed and left to the mercy of the societies in which we live. We have been forced to hide an integral part of our identity in the shadows, even within our own communities. Yes, I too felt guilty for being one who could successfully challenge the norms and cause radical changes.

My dear ones, being brilliant is a gift. Your brilliance is a component of the identity embedded in your DNA—your personal code of purpose. It was given to serve you and others, while you become all you are meant to be. You are like a star. Let's take a brief look: a star is formed within a cloud of gas. Pressure then causes the star(s) to emerge from the gas bubble and disburse into the universe. We also emerge from pressure within our mother's womb. We arrive and eventually create our own cloud. Upon arrival on earth, we all are like brilliant stars in the sky. Some shine brighter than others, but all have a place in this universe. Much like you, I was a rising star from an early age, but didn't understand that there was a purpose in my uniqueness. Although I tried, I did not fit in with my family, or crowds within my community. I often spoke out of turn (because I already had the answer) only to find myself wading in troubled waters. (Stars also have sudden outbursts called novas.) I attempted to live what is called the "dumbed down" life, but quickly discovered that I was not living, but existing. Neither gave me relief from my internal frustrations, nor hope of a future that would welcome me. Is this you? Don't give up. Remember, I stated that I was guilty, too.

We are here to shine on earth as the stars embellish the heavens. My hope for you is that you will recognize and accept that you are brilliant because of the intention of one greater than you. Fuel your glow by seeking others who desire to shine brilliantly, too. You will find peace, rest, freedom, and a greater understanding of the impact for which you were designed. However, and more significantly, I believe you will discover that you are as much a gift to them as they are to you.

Let not your light be diminished. Shine brilliantly!

With love,

Eli Thompson

Dear Brilliant One!

When I look at you, I see a smart, talented and beautiful young woman who is also an unrepeatable miracle deserving of everything she desires. I am often struck by your ability to dream big dreams, and to see a future for yourself that is filled with everything you need to succeed. Not only are you a bright, young leader, but you are an amazing daughter, sister, and friend who cares how others feel, sometimes to a fault.

And even with all of these amazing things working for you, life will happen, and you will experience moments in the wilderness where you start to question your worthiness, feel like you're not good enough, and be in a constant loop of comparing yourself to others.

You are also going to undoubtedly struggle to fit in, find friends, find your place, and find your voice and they all may very well happen at once. And you'll experience both the challenge and beauty of going through your personal rites of passage as you transition into womanhood.

Life will present you with lots of choices and whatever you do, never give away your power to choose, and always choose from a place of power. Each morning when you rise, be excited knowing that great things are in store for the future you are designing. Remember that life's obstacles are only temporary roadblocks but steeped inside of them are also lessons. Do not allow the obstacles to change your resolve, your focus, or your will to succeed. Use your brilliance, your skills and your intuition to find a way forward and around each challenge, so you can continue on the path to success. Oh, and remember that relationships are your highest form of currency; and having a trusted girl squad that you are a part of is so very important. Make a commitment to always be creating, nurturing, growing and tapping into them.

In order to achieve all that you desire, you must first believe that you deserve it, and then you must believe that you can achieve it. As I write this letter to you, I believe there is absolutely nothing that can keep you from your destiny as long as you do not become the obstacle to your success. A whole and fully expressed life is one that places a priority on your lifestyle and livelihood, relationships and contribution, creativity and learning, body and wellness, essence and spirituality. Get clear on what success feels like in each area and make it your mission to get and keep each one fulfilled. On the days when you're tired, allow yourself to rest and decompress, because self-care is the price of admission to enduring success.

See every situation as an opportunity to do or achieve something great and always embrace even the most understated opportunity by looking for the value, the lesson, and the blessing within it.

Love,

Felicia Davis

To My Dear Beautiful Black Sister,

I see you trying to raise your children more consciously and intentionally. I hear you; I feel you. I am you.

I get it. Your childhood was tough. Perhaps Daddy wasn't around much, and you watched your mother struggle to provide your basic needs. The struggles brought you two closer, but her pain also became your pain. You had to grow up quickly. You experienced so much pain in your childhood and you're still healing from things you do not discuss. I applaud you. I see your beauty, your courage, your strength, and tenacity.

Even though you know God has helped you tremendously, it's undeniable what the trauma has done to you. You have masked it beautifully, and despite the burden you carry, you are remarkably strong, even in your vulnerability. You've discovered wisdom in your wounds, and you are determined to break free from the shackles of your childhood and your past. You know that everything you went through contributed to your becoming the phenomenal woman that you are, even though you sometimes doubt your brilliance. You have realized everything that happened *to* you was happening *for* you. Your story holds the key to your authenticity and has become a survival guide for others who look up to you.

Becoming a mother has opened you up in ways you never imagined possible. Motherhood has made you view yourself and your life from a whole new perspective. You thought you knew yourself, but then you came face-to-face with the reality that your story has a direct impact on the way you parent your children. You have been presented with a choice to either recreate an environment for your children similar to your childhood, or to do things differently. You've chosen the latter, because you know how trauma can influence the trajectory of a child's life. Sis, from the bottom of my heart, I thank you for your commitment to raise children who need not recover from their childhood as adults.

It takes courage to forgive those who hurt you, either knowingly or unknowingly. It takes courage to break hard-wired destructive patterns and cycles. It takes courage to embark on a journey of healing, so you do not bleed on people who did not cut you, including your children. It takes courage to strive to become the mother your children need, so they can grow and thrive and fulfill their purpose and destiny in life. They see how hard you work on doing your best to provide them with a peaceful and love-filled home. They see how you make mistakes on your motherhood journey, and they appreciate how you work to repair any strain in your relationship with them. The deep connection, mutual respect, and unconditional love and acceptance you share with them will help them thrive and blossom beautifully.

Your brave decision to parent in a way that breaks negative cycles is worth celebrating. Having your voice in your precious children's heads means that they will have faith. They will believe in themselves, their abilities and creativity; they will have the confidence to be themselves, be proud of their authenticity and identity. They will not be afraid to make mistakes. They will live a life of meaning, purpose, and make a huge impact in this world. This is all thanks to you, sis! You did this! You are beautiful; you are brilliant, and you are enough. And you need to own it!

With love,

Britta Ofori-Kuragu

Dear Sister and Friend,

You've probably watched this scene on TV over and over: a group of doctors walk into a patient's hospital room. The senior doctor asks the interns the patient's status. An intern begins with, "The patient arrived at the hospital and presents with back pain and shortness of breath."

This scenario also happens outside of hospitals; we all present symptoms. Past experiences produce symptoms that alter our outward state. Indications of withdrawal can seep in from being minimized and dismissed; signs of defeat spill from dreams that have not come true. Symptoms hide our brilliance; yes, the very brilliance that the entire universe is standing on tiptoes yearning to see. Your brilliance is designed for others to enjoy.

In this letter, I am contextualizing brilliance as an intellectually curious person. Brilliant people are curious learners, journeyers and seekers. Brilliant people wake up to a blank check each morning. They understand that each day is a story only they can write.

Learning creates authority. Facts trump fiction, truth trumps falsehood, and authenticity trumps flaws. An intellectually curious person is not always the most favored person. In our youth, we learn to avoid wise guys and smart alecks. That is, we are taught to shun truth. In our best efforts to live an accomplished life, circumstances occur that are human-made traps, and let's face it, self-induced outcomes.

In so, let us not conflate experiences with truth. Identifying truth is an art form in seeking understanding. Sojourner Truth is quoted as saying, "Truth is powerful and it prevails." A master astronomist and brilliant Black man, Neil Degrasse Tyson, taught that there are three kinds of truth: personal truth, political truth, and objective truth. Objective truth is where brilliance lives; where we allow ourselves to learn and evolve. When you commit to evolve your understanding, it matters less how others interpret your brilliance.

Dear one, I encourage you to continue to ask questions, challenge the status quo, and dispute the interpretation of your personal experiences. I am standing on tip-toes yearning to see your brilliance; in headlines, in corporate leadership, in government, in social support, or wherever your calling leads. Your brilliance is the fabric of creation—and you are to be enjoyed.

Lovingly,

Rachelle Byars-Sargent

Dear Daughter,

Here are some things I wish I knew; things I wish someone had told me when I was young, figuring out how to forge my way and create a life I could enjoy. The first thing I had to learn was that I am brilliant. I was uniquely created on purpose. Every part of who I am was created on purpose.

I hope I can pass on some perspective that helps you see that you are brilliant! Brilliance comes in many forms, so worry not if you don't fit into the box established by current culture. Just know that your brilliance is special—uniquely yours. Once you believe this, you will shine brighter. When stars shine bright or diamonds gleam of light, they are often described as brilliant. Why not you? Your laugh, your freckles, the shape of your lips, your quick wit. Your indescribable love for words, or music or cooking or nature. That's part of your brilliance. Don't hide it. Own it. Respect it. Love it, genuinely. Once you do, others will, too.

As a preschool-aged girl, my parents were often told there were things about my character and personality that would be great when I became an adult. My sass. My incessant need to understand. Even four-year-old me needed things to make sense in order for me to follow a directive. Now as a parent, I completely understand how my parents and teachers gritted their teeth in frustration. Still, as a parent, I completely understand why the questions of a child are evidence of their brilliance in its infancy. You see, we don't become a mature, reasonable, rational adult when our chronological age reaches 18 or 21. No, we mature through a process of nature and nurture experiences. The same goes for our brilliance. That inquisitive little girl would grow to become a member of corporate leadership teams in environments that insisted on confidence in her abilities, awareness of her shortcomings, and a large dose of respect for others and herself. The many years between preschool and corporate America were foundational. She had to have adults who would not be threatened by her need to understand things she certainly lacked the experience and wisdom to understand.

What about you? Are you letting your brilliance shine? Are you a woman feeling conflicted about how you wear your hair? Your creative ability to go from hair extensions to styling your short or thinning or otherwise not so photo-shoot-ready hair; that's part of your brilliance. Not everyone has the eye to pull it off. What do you bring to the table in your career? Are your ideas in your head or in a journal, instead of voiced in meetings with colleagues or bosses?

Do you have a daughter who makes you think to yourself, "This will be a great character trait when she is older?" Allow me to challenge you to see the beauty in it now. Maybe your daughter needs a little molding of how she asks her questions. If so, what a beautiful opportunity for you to nurture the brilliance already inside of her. If you are not yet a mother, pour that energy into yourself. Do the work in you, then find a young woman who needs you to pour into her.

You matter. You are brilliant. Let your light shine.

With Love,

Nichole K. Sullivan

Dear Sisters,

Did you bury your hope so deep that it lost its meaning in your life? Did you hide your purpose behind those curtains because you got stage fright? What about your dreams? Are they still disguised as stars only to be seen at night? Where is your new thing? Yeah, that thing that gets you excited. Bring that to light!

I am truly convinced that Black women possess this special imperishable courage that miraculously appears when they get knocked down. Then, as fast as you can blink your eyes, she's back up, through and over it. There's not a day that goes by that I don't see a Black woman struggling to overcome something. And, I can't help but get excited with joy when she overcomes, because to me it feels the same as watching a bad scene in a movie make a turn for the good. But as a sister, I know it's hard being us, and the expectation of strength can weigh heavy on our shoulders. This is why I strongly felt the need to write this letter and to encourage you to push through your failures, no matter how defeating the situation may feel.

Success is no easy task, and sometimes I wanted to walk away from my dreams. Through my ups and downs, I've come to believe that a situation is only as bad as you perceive it. When you direct your focus to the positive aspects of an uncomfortable situation, then, and only then, can you heal and problem-solve. Therefore, you must always make the difficult choice to keep going, to stay focused and keep a positive mental state.

When I was young, my father would always say "Wisdom is the byproduct of fearlessness." It took me 45 years to understand what he meant, and to accept that this world is not a pretty place; painful setbacks will happen. That's why we must be courageous in our faith, my sisters. I remind myself constantly that we have a deep history of surviving the worse that this life has offered. We have endured; yet are still vulnerable and unprotected. Even today, we're still enduring varying forms of disparities in our country, yet we still shine the brightest in any room we enter.

I wholeheartedly believe that God has a thing for us, and it is special! Because it is only through His acts of divine intervention that we are able to still shine like diamonds. Sisters, I encourage you to do your thing, fearlessly! Show the world that you legitimately belong in the fastest-growing population in this nation to own businesses, earn college degrees, and gain political positions. God is with us and that is why we must be proud of the innate strengths we inherited from the great souls that came before us. Allow God to guide you. With His guidance, you'll learn how to eliminate distracting uncertainties, fears, worries, and failures, and be able to overcome your adversities like our mothers, grandmothers, great-grandmothers, and their mothers.

With love,

Janella Dobbs

...Beautiful

To My Amazing Black Daughter,

We live in a world where beauty is both desired and despised, revered and reviled. Beauty gets you noticed, but your spirit—your being (your soul) is the true source of your exquisiteness. We have been taught to see beauty in others, but they consider it vanity when we recognize beauty in ourselves, or we desire to be beautiful. This, my dear, could not be further from the truth.

Beauty is not about trying to achieve or exceed the mainstream standards and expectations of others. Your real beauty captivates and draws people to you because of how you make them feel. Take back your power; beauty is not in the eye of the beholder—the observer does not get to decide what is beautiful. You do! Beauty is defined through your eyes.

As a mother, I hope you were raised to know how beautiful you are, and to recognize the beauty in others; to help our sisters see the beauty in them. Today I affirm that you are blessed, melanated, brilliant, textured, shapely, bodacious, and all that makes you beautiful.

Find beauty in nature—your natural beauty.

Find beauty in smiles—give and receive them.

Find beauty in your boldness—and if they do not give you a seat at the table, bring your sovereign throne, Young Queen.

With love forever, shine bright like the diamond you are,

Kiana Romeo

Dear Love,

Just in case no one told you today, you are beautiful! I don't mean the superficial beauty society will have us believe is the standard or norm. I don't mean the beauty that says you have to weigh this much; your hair has to be this long, or your skin has to be that complexion. I'm not talking about the beauty that can be seen with the naked eye. No! I'm talking about the beauty that is in your soul. The beauty that can be found from within. The beauty that doesn't have to be validated by anyone but you. Honey, you are beautiful!

Your spirit is beautiful, your strength is beautiful, and your resilience is be-you-til-full! In all your splendor, you shine bright like the gem you are. The pressure you have endured throughout life has made you into a beautiful diamond. You are rare! You bring value to this world just by being you. You heal the world with your power, your energy, and your story. Herstory. In the words of poet Useni Eugene Perkins, "Hey, black child! Do you know who you are? Who you really are?" You are the mother of the first man. Your past is rooted in excellence. You are magic! Exquisite. Your Blackness does not hinder you from being beautiful; truth be told, you are beautiful because of your Blackness.

Sweetie; define beauty for yourself. If beauty is in the eye of the beholder, take a look in the mirror and behold the beauty of who you are. Focusing on society's false definition of beauty will have you thinking you are not good enough and discounting your worth and value. But, sista! You are the truth! You are good and you are beautiful just the way you are. Believe it! Make the mirror your best friend. It will help you accept yourself; flawed, yet phenomenal. Embrace the shape of your nose, eyes, lips, ears and cheekbones. Embrace the width of your hips. You are not the number on the scale. Tell yourself, "I am beautiful!"

The Higher Power makes no mistakes! The same power that created the stars, sunrise and sunset, oceans and seas, mountains and valleys, also created you. You were intricately and uniquely made with purpose. No one else is quite like you and that is where your power lies. It doesn't matter what he says about you, or what she thinks about you. What do you say and think about you? The words *ugly* and *Black Woman* cannot rightly coexist in the same sentence. The Black woman is beauty; in all her different shapes, shades and ages. You are the epitome of beauty. Don't believe it? Let me tell you what beautiful is. Beautiful is a state of being. It is being breathtaking, evolved, able, unapologetic, tenacious, innovative, fabulous, unshakeable, and lovable. Queen, you are beautiful. Beautiful is being Black, elegant, attentive, unique, triumphant, intelligent, fearless, unbothered, and legendary. Yes, you are beautiful!

Do you know why it hurts so much when you try to fit into society's box? Because you were not born to fit in. You are limitless, infinite, and you were born to stand out! So, live out loud—unapologetically. We are all reflections of one another! If I am beautiful, you are beautiful. If she is beautiful, you are beautiful. We, my queen, are all beautiful.

Love,

Trici Coleman

Dear Beautiful Black Daughter,

You are amazing and beautiful. Often in our society, there will be moments when you find it hard to see the beauty you possess. You will see so many ideas of what "beauty" is, and many of the ideas won't look like you. Does this mean that your beautiful brown, chocolate skin is unattractive? Absolutely not! You possess an inner and outer beauty that some fear, and many others will pay for. You are beautiful!

Your skin is the perfect shade and the exact way God intended! You walk into the room and immediately people notice you for your outer beauty; the way that you carry yourself, and your mannerisms. But what really draws them closer is your intellect. You are beautiful and brilliant, and it blows people away.

Life is going to throw you drama and when it comes your way, you might not know how to handle it or have a difficult time figuring out what to do next. But, baby girl, I promise, you might sulk for a little while, but you will figure out how to get through it and you will come out on the other side in victory.

Relationships will be another maze that you must maneuver through. You will get hurt, you will feel like life is over, and that you will never love another soul like that again; but I promise, "This too shall pass." Take the time to learn who you are. Learn all the things you like, don't like, can tolerate, and just have no time for and move from that space. Accept nothing less, because you are beautiful. As you grow within your relationship, never forget who you are, and don't dim your light for anyone. Relationships can be testy, but once you battle through those tough times, you heal and begin dating again. You will see that there is a beautiful love waiting for you on the other side. It's there; patiently waiting for you because you are beautiful!

Your care and concern for others is so admirable. You see someone in need and try to help in whatever way you can. Mothers will always want what they think is best for their daughters—but the reality is, daughters might want to choose what they think is best for themselves. I commend you for just being you. You stand in your own purpose and live according to your own terms. You remain respectful, but you allow your life to be lived in the way you want. You stand tall in your decisions and that inner beauty you possess exudes onto those around you. You are beautiful!

Shine bright, dream big and live your purpose, beautiful daughter. Stand in your beauty and allow no one to tell you otherwise. You are beautiful!

Love,

Jamie Newton-Knight

To My Beautiful Black Sisters,

For years you have been told or at least presented with a concept of what is beautiful. Ads, television, and even dolls you played with as a child lacked diverse images of beauty. I think we could agree society has defined its ideology of what is beautiful. This beauty of what is seen is superficial, and often conceals the true beauty found in our mélange of skin tones, shapes and hair textures.

The fickleness of society's definition of beautiful has been illustrated time and time again, as we witness what they consider beautiful constantly changing. For example, Black women are criticized for having big butts, big lips, skin too dark and nappy hair, as though how we naturally look is society's definition of ugly. If that were true, would we see women of all ethnicities getting injections to achieve the look of our naturally endowed big butts and big lips? Would tanning salons be a multi-billion-dollar industry? And I don't know about you, but I come across countless white men and women with dreadlocks. They spend a lot of money to emulate our beauty. The point is, you were created exactly the way you should look—perfect!

Now that you have been enlightened on the concept of physical beauty, forever changing and always subjective; I introduce to you another dimension of beauty—the beauty within. How we see ourselves and others is often the result of physical or emotional experiences we've encountered. I am writing you this love letter to share some important life lessons I have learned along my journey.

First, accept all of who you are and recognize that you are a significant—yet a singular—part of something greater than yourself. Over time, you'll learn that the things you boldly show the world are only as important as the things about yourself you try to conceal from the world. With this awareness, you'll come to understand that you were created exactly how you were supposed to be, and you have the power to control who you become. In your strength, you offer part of you that contributes to the whole; and in your weakness, you are able to humble yourself to receive from the whole.

Second, recognize that someone considering you to be ugly results from their brokenness—not because you are ugly, unworthy or unloved. This will help you transform from being a victim into a powerful woman who recognizes that your true beauty is within, which will enhance your physical beauty. Try tuning into your inner being where you are free and able to recognize, receive and release that which you do not wish to be part of your being. Exercise the ritual of reciting "I am" affirmations you have yet to master. Using this practice helped me to become who I have affirmed myself to be.

In closing, I ask you, my beautiful sister, to begin your days with your positive affirmations. Look in the mirror and tell yourself, "I am beautiful." Recite your affirmation until you have become it, and once you become it, choose another set of affirmations. For example: "I am bold," or "I am confident." Every day you are transforming into your tomorrow self, so keep affirming that you are beautiful, and celebrate your beauty with your head held high, and move forward.

With love,

Diane Renee

Dear Black Woman,

Do you realize how beautiful you are? Do you realize the magnitude of your beauty? Do you realize the lineage you started based on your beauty? Do you know that you are the first and the last? If you answered these questions without hesitation, then Black woman, this letter is for you. I call this "If Beauty Is A Curse, Then I Don't Need A Blessing."

How do I see the beauty of you? Let me count the many ways. Black woman, your beauty was created when Mother Nature decided who would follow in her image. She concocted a formula of natural ingredients using oxygen, carbon, hydrogen and nitrogen; but our Big Sista didn't stop there. Mother Nature, on her throne, in her spiritual lab, put together other ingredients. She knew this woman could never be basic. She knew this mysterious woman needed the most powerful things added to her makeup to produce the most beautiful woman in the world. Mother Nature knew what she needed. She knew that this special woman must have gifts others would want and possibly die for. Mother knew she needed the thing that engulfs everything; what you say, how you perform, how you think and how you breathe. While in her lab, she combined these powerful ingredients to finish her product. She used a cup of power, a cup of strength, and three cups of inner and outer melanated beauty. The woman she created is you!

Black woman, you epitomize the magnitude of womanhood. Once created, Mother Nature took a step back and brought you before God, and they were both well-pleased. Beautiful Black Woman, this woman is you. Mother Nature gave you the beauty of melanin and strength. Your melanin is the sensual part of your being and existence in this universe. It forms you; it shapes you, molds you and directs you in ways others cannot. It defines your beauty. It defines your strength, your vulnerability, your strategy, and your divine power. Your beauty provides a glowing aura that says to the world, "I cannot be moved," and "I will not stand down." Your beauty makes men pause, even though some will never let you see their lingering glance. Your beauty is everlasting. It shines in the brightness of the boardroom and in the iridescence of the bedroom. It shifts mindsets, and it enhances the curiosity of others. Your beauty is of the sun, because the sun has a special love for you. You have been deeply kissed by the sun; your skin absorbs the sun's rays when it stretches its arms around you. Like a hurricane, your beauty generates energy to move swiftly in protests and boycotts when our Black and Brown bodies are devalued and destroyed.

Because of your natural beauty, people will mock you, poke fun and bully you—yet still try to replicate you and copy everything, from your broad lips and your broad nose to your curves. Black woman, the original is always more beautiful, delicate, and intricate than the counterfeit. Your beauty is so unique that your DNA is seen in everyone you encounter.

Black Woman, love your beauty, embrace your beauty, and show your beauty, because your beauty was custom created by Mother Nature and approved by God.

Your sista in love,

Dr. Zakia Y. Gates

Hi Girls,

Have you ever heard of the words *beauty* or *beautiful*? I know I have. Don't you love when you wake up in the morning and you see the sun shining? It's beautiful, isn't it? There is so much beauty in the world, and you are part of what makes the world beautiful. Don't change who you are. Be you! Be yourself!

If someone says you are ugly, who cares? You know it's not true. Next thing you know, you want to change who you are. See how someone's words can change you? Don't pay attention to that person. Be you! Be yourself!

Has anyone told you how beautiful you are? Well if not, too bad for them, because you are beautiful. You are amazing. You are you. You are important. Don't let anybody tell you differently, and even if they do, just ignore them. Remember these words and remember the good in you. Be you, be yourself!

I remember learning in school about a time when some Black people would change the color of their skin, just so they could be treated like white people were treated; like human beings. They wanted to feel beautiful and to be treated better. I understand why they did it, but I still don't think people should change who they are to fit someone else's standards of beauty. Do you see how what people say and do can make you want to change who you really are? Always be you!

I remember one time when I didn't feel beautiful. It was last year when my friend accidentally scratched me on my back. It left an enormous red mark. The bad part of the situation was that I was at my dance recital and was the next one to perform on stage. I was panicking. I thought if I went on stage, everyone in the audience would see this big, ugly red mark on my back. But if I stayed backstage, no one would see it, and I wouldn't be embarrassed.

Even though the red scratch was on my back, I still felt less beautiful. It felt ugly, and it hurt. I didn't want to go on stage; I was too scared. I didn't want anyone to laugh at me or point out that mark. I was also thinking however, that I couldn't let my dance team down. I said to myself, "Malayah Rahman never lets her team down." So, I went on stage and performed with my team. I can't believe I almost let something as little as a scratch get in the way of dancing and cause me to let my team down. I still have a scar from that scratch, and I still keep dancing. Do you see how the tiniest things can sometimes get in the way of you succeeding in life or having fun? We can still be beautiful and do great things, even when we have scars from past hurts. Don't let the bad things change who you are or make you feel less beautiful. Be you! Be yourself!

I hope by now you are feeling beautiful, because you are! You don't need makeup or things to cover up your face or your scars to be beautiful. All you need is to be you. You are already beautiful just the way you are. Be the best you can be by just being yourself. Be you!

Love,

Malayah Rahman

...Strong

Dear Beautiful Black Queen,

You are strong! No matter what your mind tells you, you've got this! Strength comes in many forms, but I want to share my thoughts on the strength that exists in being true to yourself, looking inward, and asking for help.

Be true to yourself. In the superficial world we live in, all you see are comparisons and the next "in" thing to do, see, or even look like. But where is the diversity in all of it? Life is filled with multi-faceted women, and our individuality should be amplified and celebrated, not compared to one another, or judged and made to feel less than. Our strength is in our differences and how we show up. You'll receive more of what you want in life by showing up just as you are. And while it's okay to look up to other women—even famous women—now is the time to walk strong in knowing who you are so people look up to you! So, put down your tablet or phone, and open your heart to yourself.

Look inwardly. Some of you may not know who you are or what you want to give to the world. I recommend you search inside of yourself to find your gift. True strength lies in knowing your gift and in the journey of discovery. Know that the gifts in you are ever evolving. As you grow, change and learn, your gifts will develop and expand. There's no right or wrong gift. And whatever your gift is, it will align with who you are and what you're innately passionate about—the things that truly matter to you. So, take some time to sit in a quiet place and listen to the voice within you. Whether it's through meditation, prayer, chanting or whatever you do to tune in to your spirit; do so, and listen to the response. It may surprise you, scare you, or both. Either way, it'll tell you what you need to do next. You'll be eternally thankful.

Ask for help. There's so much strength in seeking help because we are not all-knowing. Even if we think we are, we're not! There's strength in seeking out those who can get us closer to the next step of our calling. Sometimes as Black women, we think we can be everything to everyone we care for the most. But we don't stop to think of who can be there for us, and that is to our detriment. Seek professional help to heal inwardly first. Then, seek a mentor to help you professionally or in an area you want to learn more about. Ask someone to be your moral support or your sounding board during this quest. There's strength in knowing you're not on this journey alone. Your higher power will not leave you in any stage of life without support. Your greatest strength is found in acknowledging and getting help for your weaknesses.

Walk in the glory of who you are, always check in with yourself to ensure you're aligned with your true purpose, and know you have support from fellow sistas to cheer you on and guide you throughout life. We need you my Queen, and we're all waiting for you to take your throne.

With love and strength,

India Thomas-Johns

My Daughter, My Sister, My Friend,

You are strong and created to win. To be strong is to manifest courage. You don't just become strong; you choose to become strength. It is a way of being. If you are being, you are doing. It takes a lot to be strong with what life throws at you; but you my sister, daughter and friend, are made perfect in strength.

Not everyone will recognize your strength unless they see it displayed through courage. When they see you walking with your head held high and your shoulders back after the world just hit you upside your head, you are being strong. When you stand tall and smile and no one knows the hell you've been through at home or work, you are still being strong. Having the courage to move forward when everything you see tells you to stop, fall back or quit takes strength.

My sister, you were created with everything you need inside of you to be strong—to actively move forward in your moments of weakness. Your thoughts, actions and words can paint a portrait of your strength. When life happens, is happening, or has happened not the way you desired, your next steps are powered by your strength. You move forward, whether you feel like it or not. Think about it. Compare the number of times you chose to be strong against the times you chose to be weak. I bet your strong times win over your weak times. That's because you are strong.

Don't allow yourself to be a victim of circumstances designed to break you. Choose to be an overcomer. Choose to achieve greatness. Choose to stand upright and shine bright. Choose to win! To be strong is not being perfect or having it all together. It is not going it alone or refusing help. Sometimes being strong is knowing when and how to take a break from the fight. Sometimes it's allowing the tears to flow from your eyes, even when people are watching. Sometimes it's talking to yourself, about yourself, by yourself so you can come to yourself. Sometimes it's asking for help and talking to someone else; but be careful, make sure they can hold your dirty dishwater. Sometimes strength looks like total submission to someone or something you don't want to submit to; giving up your right to be right, or choosing to lose so someone else can win. That's being strong!

Strong you were created to be, and strong is what you are. Don't think about what happened to you. Don't focus on what they said about you. Be strong and courageous enough to focus on what's in front of you. I know you won't always feel strong, or even feel like being strong. When those times come, use your words to speak what is not into existence. Joel 3:10 (NKJV) says, "Let the weak say, I am strong." Use your mouth as a propeller to eradicate your feelings of weakness. Call those things that rise up against you to threaten the power within you into subjection to your strength. My daughter, my sister, my friend. You are strong. You have creative power within you gifted by the One who created you. Be who you were created to be. Be strong!

Love you,

Trina Vessels

To My Beautiful Sister!

First, allow me to say you are strong, beautiful and bold. A rich piece of dark, delicious chocolate! You are sweet, sensual and desirable. You have a force working on the inside of you that is bigger than you and I could possibly imagine. You are fearfully and wonderfully made. It's time you release the childhood hurts and pain that you've held onto for so long. All of those negative thoughts that have kept you in bondage—let them go! It's time to get to know the new, improved you! There's a superwoman inside of you, screaming to be free. Embrace her and become the person you were created to be.

When you look in the mirror, what do you see? You may say you see yourself as someone who can't seem to get it together. That my dear, is a lie straight from the pit of hell! You are strong, resilient, and powerful. You have no idea how many young women look up to you and admire you. You may say, "You don't know what I've been through, or what I'm going through now." You are not alone! I've been there, and so have many other women. You will win because you are a winner! The greater One lives on the inside of you, and you were made to win.

As you read this letter, realize everything starts with you and your attitude. What is in your mouth? Are you speaking words of life, building your strength up, or tearing yourself down and bringing defeat? Once we realize death and life are in the power of our tongue, then and only then can we claim life, strength, power, and even wealth. Our strength comes from within—or should I say, from our own words.

Whatever life may throw you, create an atmosphere of positivity and look for the good in people. Demonstrate what it looks like to overcome. You may not realize you have so many young sisters looking up to you. Trust me, people are looking at you. Young women are looking for strong, independent role models. Why not you? Don't take that lightly, it's an awesome responsibility. Never give up! Sometimes you have to encourage yourself; but you are never alone. You have so many sisters praying for you, rooting for you, and wanting to see you thrive!

Now, take another look in the mirror and see what I see. A strong, beautiful, humble, courageous source to be reckoned with! Know that you are made in the image of God. When I think of you, I think of a lotus flower. A lotus flower is a symbol of purity, enlightenment, self-regeneration, and rebirth. Its characteristics are a perfect analogy for human conditions. Even when its roots are in the dark muddy waters, the lotus produces the most beautiful flower. So, I say to you "Rise, lotus flower, rise."

Peace and love,

Janett V. Blanchard

Dear Black Girl,

My name is Aja, and I am also a Black girl. It is an honor that you chose my letter to read. I just want to take a few lines to dive into your life's journey; the past, present and beautiful future. We all need someone to lean on. We all need support and guidance, especially from our sisters. I am here for you always, whether in the form of a letter, phone call, or in person—you say the word. I want you to internalize this letter and become the best version of yourself. Be Strong.

Black girl, you continue to smile through your pain and respond "I'm okay" when asked how you are doing. It is okay to be strong; in fact, I admire that about you. While being strong, it is important that you are honest with yourself, and not tell the world you are "fine" so often that you believe it yourself. It is okay to be strong and not okay.

You have encountered countless heartaches over the years. The traumas you experienced would have easily broken most people—but you are not most people, are you? The hardships that were designed to break you; you carried them over your shoulder like a bag of laundry and continued to soar like the eagle you are. I don't believe you chose to be assigned the burden of strength, but strength chose you. You did not choose to be the family member to always have things together, "the perfect Black girl," yet it often feels like you are the key to holding your family together.

Sometimes you want to stop all movement in the world and just leave, right? Fly away like the caged bird you are. Yes, caged. That is what I see when I look at you. "Caged" is not a negative description. You continually knock down the bars blocking you to step over those barriers and break free. Young, beautiful woman, you are unstoppable and physically, mentally, spiritually, and emotionally free from the cage when you accept it, get the map, formulate your escape plan, and direct your future; because only you know where that journey leads.

It is time for you to deal with your internal hurt or I fear it will deal with you. I know what it's like to keep yourself busy 24 hours a day, seven days a week to avoid dealing with your past trauma. I also know that avoidance tactics will only work for so long before anxiety and depression disrupt your daily activities. Before you know it, you'll be paralyzed with fear, paranoid of losing someone else, and find yourself emotionally and physically caged. This is where that heartache will lead you if you don't deal with it.

It is okay to not be okay. You were born with a heart to help any and everyone who comes across your path, but who is helping you? Even with several support systems, the bulk of the load is still on you because no one knows you like you. You know what you need. Not doctors, society, social workers, or anyone else. What do you need? Black girl, I want you to be the best you possible. I want you to surpass the stars and live the dreams you desire. Let me rephrase that last statement; you will surpass the stars, and you will live the dreams you desire.

I admire you. I love you and I believe in you. Be strong, Black Queen.

Aja K. Ellington

My Beautiful Daughter,

As I was sitting here thinking, the thought came across my mind to share with you what I see in you. Sometimes you don't believe you have enough in you to take on the next tasks or challenges coming your way. Sometimes you question your ability to pace yourself in the wake of change and adversity, but you have so much more in you than what you can see. You have an inner strength that always rises to the occasion to seize the moment. Don't cower in fear. Be strong! I see you facing your challenges instead of running from them, even though you don't know how things will turn out. The best thing you've done through the ripples of tests and trials was to show up, anyway. In showing up, a greater power in you embraced the opportunity for another conquest.

You're questioning yourself now, wondering if you have enough stamina for the race you're in. The answer is yes; without question, you do. Remember that the strength your lungs have is the capacity to take another breath; inhale, exhale. In your downtime you learned to breathe through it all. You learned that it's okay to relax when the calmness comes, and that it's important to speak words of encouragement to yourself. I see you training your thoughts to be words of power and positivity. I see you harnessing your emotions so you can think clearly and make coordinated moves. I see you making decisions that capture the essence of the quiet, yet powerful strength you possess. Even still, sometimes during these great victories, you question yourself, "Am I strong enough, because I sure don't feel like I am?" You are strong enough. Don't cower in fear. Be strong!

I am here to remind you of how smart, beautiful and strong you are. Never compare yourself to other people because no two people are the same, nor do they respond the same way to the same situation. One beauty of your strength is your faith. Your faith will carry you a long way in life and your faith is the wind that gives flight to your being, refreshes your soul, and establishes the cadence of your heart. You are a hard worker, and it shows in everything you set your mind to do. You'll often feel underappreciated, but don't let that rob you of your virtue. This has a way of changing your trajectory. You are strong enough to snatch it and send it in the intended direction.

Whatever feelings you have while experiencing the frustration that comes with uncertainty, express it in a non-damaging way. Scream, if you need to. Take your energy to the gym and work off your anxiety or negative energy. Cry if you need to. Even the strongest people cry sometimes. It doesn't diminish who you are as a person, and it is not a sign of weakness. Every one of your tears is counted and used to further mold you into the person you are meant to become. I believe in you, and here is why: I've learned things about myself in watching you overcome the struggles and hurdles of life. I've learned that when you think you cannot raise your leg to scale another hurdle, you run towards it anyway, and allow the wind of faith to be the strength that raises your leg at the right interval. My daughter; be strong.

Love,

Annette Jackson

My Dear Sister,

"You never know how strong you are until being strong is the only choice you have."
—Bob Marley

This has been my favorite quote ever since I first heard it. It speaks volumes. It explains how tough moments separate individuals who quit from individuals who never give up. It recognizes that our worst experiences reveal the heart and courage that exists inside of you. Think about it. Every time bad things happen; we question *why* or *why me*. But in our toughest moments, we see who people really are. We see who we really are. Sometimes we have to go through things to understand how truly blessed we are.

Can I share my story to illustrate a lesson? I am a walking testimony. I died at birth and was resuscitated by the doctors. I grew up to be the biggest, darkest and nerdiest person in the class, but also the youngest, which made me the school joke. After listening to the jokes for so long, I started to believe their words were true. I had no self-esteem. Whenever someone wanted to talk to me, I questioned their motives. I then did whatever they wanted to keep them around because I wanted to feel wanted. I spent ten years of my life in an abusive relationship, almost dying twice.

Over the past two years, I became very ill. Then my husband died, and I lost my job, my car, and my home. I was in a major depression which resulted in me losing everything—including myself. I even lost a few people who I thought had my back and best interests at heart. It took me losing everything to realize my strength, my worth and my purpose; and I cherish the lesson I learned in the process. I learned that I am stronger than I ever imagined. I remember thinking I was weak, nothing, ugly, helpless, and not enough. I even tried to take my life, but here I am. I know that I am strong!

My sister, hear me and feel the power of my words when I say that you are strong. Your story may be different from mine, but I know you have a story. I know you have survived the worst moments in your life. How do I know? You are still here. Sister, you are strong! There will be times when you fall in life, and some falls will be harder than others. The truth is, everyone falls—but only the strong get back up. Sister, you are strong, so "Be strong and courageous! Do not be afraid or discouraged. For the Lord your God is with you wherever you go" (Joshua 1:9 NLT). This verse reminds me that I am never alone because God is always with me, and because He is with me, I am strong, and I can be courageous. I don't know if you've ever heard this verse or if you believe it, but I hope it encourages you. Sister; move courageously forward in this uncertain world knowing that even in your weakest moments, you are strong. Strong enough to survive. Choose to survive. You are not alone. As your sister, I am always here. Be strong!

Love,

Nydia S. Wells-Evans

Section Two

BE...

...Yourself

Dear Black Women,

I love you. I love you because I am you and I feel your pain. I understand your uniqueness comes with a heavy price imposed by society. The burdens you carry are unknown by other women. They don't see the world as you do; they don't feel your pain, and they will never understand the complexities of the Black experience. I am here to tell you that this is okay.

Embrace that we are one human family. Within this oneness you will find over a billion people with over a billion perceptions of the world. With unique perceptions come unique experiences and stories. Societal limitations happen to be a part of your story. Yet, your story does not have to be one of violent protests or cries for understanding on social media. You do not need validation of who you are from those who lack love, compassion and understanding. It is not your responsibility to change the mindset of those who do not understand we are all connected in spirit. Each person is responsible for their own knowledge and ignorance.

No longer allow their ignorance to contribute to your unhappiness and suffering. People who express hate in various forms are hurt people. Hurt people hurt people, who in turn hurt people. If they were happy and aligned with their true power and purpose, they would understand that hurting one hurts all. Don't attempt to change the mindset of human beings who wish to remain in the darkness of ignorance. You will not win this battle because this isn't your battle to fight. If a person comes to realize the oneness of humanity, it's because they made a personal and conscious decision to move toward the light of knowledge and truth. As a Black woman, you must be a light and realize your own power to end the cycle of pain in your home, with your men, children, friends, co-workers and all those who cross your path.

Your future is created by the efforts you make today. What you confront today is the result of a past you cannot change. Separatism, racism, classism, colorism and the many ways we divide are deeply rooted in the past. An annihilation of these social constructs isn't in sight. The law of this world requires good and evil to co-exist. Suffering and unhappiness come from your inability to accept this truth. Once you accept this, you begin to forgive and find your power. Your power isn't in angry, militant actions that further divide the human family. These tactics have never worked, and they fail to effectively address the pain. There's no "us" and "them," in this healing process, only the ignorant and the wise.

The wise Black woman is emotionally mature about the ways of the world and gracefully accepts this—not with anger, but with a healthy, dignified attitude. An attitude that comes from realizing that finding your power will encompass some pleasant and unpleasant experiences. For most, the journey is more unpleasant than pleasant. This makes you unique. If your story was filled with all joy and no pain, you wouldn't have the desire to find your power and the purpose designed for you.

The greatest gift you could give yourself and society is finding your power and purpose. When you're fully immersed in your true, authentic self, you show up for yourself. You respond to injustice instead of reacting to injustice. You gain confidence in your intuition and know that whatever your Higher Power places before you will lead to deeper truths and contribute to your unique story.

In purpose and power,

Nicoli Rena Sinclair

Dear Beautiful Black Queen,

Did you know that was your identity when you were born? Did you know that you don't need to be approved, justified, or simplified in any way, shape or form? Who you are is exactly who you were created to be, and your authenticity is what makes you unique. Your greatest mystery lies within your complexity. With your many shades of melanin, you are designed to shine in everything! Don't you ever shrink back, be intimidated, or extinguish your fight. Keep showing the world more of you. You ignite so bright, and we all need your light.

Precious time is wasted when you start to compare; take it from me. I've spent many nights there. "I wish I looked like her. I wish I did that like they did, or went to that place, too." I was duped into believing those falsehoods were true. I boxed myself into a corner of conformity that hurt me inside. A caged bird never flies, and with each passing moment, pieces of me died. Thus, I am writing to you—my beautiful Black queen, these words of affirmation that so many of you need.

Who exactly are you? Let's peel back the layers and unpack your intricate parts.

You are all the colors of browns and reds with hints of gold tones, warm almond hues set against backdrops of beautiful bronzes and bold blacks. The skin you're in is not easily matched. In fact, I'd dare say you are your own complexion, a one-of-a-kind batch. I so love that about you, and you should, too!

You are deserving of living in your truth, the fruit of your youth is built from strong foundational roots. You are not easily swayed, nor do you follow the crowd. You are a leader of multi-proportions because you live life out loud. Pretentious you are not by any means; your authenticity flows through. Your confidence shows forth in everything about you. Your soul is so pure, it is so hard to ignore that being yourself opens the door. Your core is the greatest. Explore. And what you discover can't be dictated, recreated, determined or violated by others. What power that is, my beautiful Black queens, to be released from comparison is freedom indeed.

To be yourself is to love yourself, flaws and all. Love the self you used to be, because you evolved. Love the self you are today, because the best place to be is present, and love the self you are becoming because that self has no limits! To love yourself is the most unselfish gift you can give that adds to the world's greatness. A loved self is allowing the human in you the ability to just be; and that, my dear sweet queen, is exactly why you were created!

All my love,

Danita L. Mosley

Beautiful Black Girl,

"You are the light of the world—like a city on a hilltop that cannot be hidden" (Matthew 5:14 NLT). You are the epitome of love. You care. You grieve. You empathize. You care so much about the world, and often think about how you can make it a better place. So, why do you shy away? Why are you so afraid to make people feel uncomfortable? Why are you afraid that people will believe you think you are better than they are? Does the vision God placed in your heart scare you? Are you afraid of stepping into who you were created to be?

Close your beautiful eyes, imagine and experience all that God promised you. Explore the journey as you transform into the authentic, impactful you! Don't be afraid! Don't ask how! Don't ask why! Trust the plan for you.

Be yourself. Be yourself for all the girls who came before you who shine bright like diamonds. Be yourself for all the girls who couldn't shine because her diamond was buried under dirt and rubbish. Be yourself for this present moment, because in this moment is where you'll find your peace of heaven on earth. Most importantly, be yourself for the girls who will come after you and through you. You are a portal to success. So, be you!

Lovingly,

Nicole A. Johnson

Girl!

Sit up straight. You talk too much. Be still. You're so light. You're ugly. These were some of the words I heard at a young age that caused me to consider myself less than, and live a life focused on pleasing others. All I wanted was to be accepted and loved. Whatever I was told to do, I did it. I always wondered why life was so difficult for me. Why was it so hard for people to see me?

What I didn't realize at the time, was that I was creating an alternative life for myself that went against the true essence of who I was. It took me years to realize I wanted more! I wanted to live a different life. I was 40 years old when I came to know myself. It all started with me reminding myself of who I was. Going back to the little girl inside of me who once dreamed, dared to be different and was curious about life. Sis, I don't want it to take you a lifetime to realize that you want more; to recognize that you deserve more.

As you continue to grow and figure out what you want to become and how you want to live, choose to be yourself. Don't be the person everyone else thinks you should be. Don't live the life everyone else wants you to live. Find out who you are—who you really are, then be her. She is magnificent! Her magnificence exists even when she is hurt, when the people she loves don't love her, and when she doesn't fit in. She is magnificent!

Be the woman you desire to be. You are more powerful, courageous and brave when you focus on being you. There's no need to waste time, energy or money trying to be someone you're not. Life is much easier just being yourself.

This is why you were born; God wanted you here. Don't wait until you're older in life to discover the real you. Don't wait until tragedy happens to realize you've been wasting time. Don't let another day go by living life for other people.

It's time for you to be more of yourself. That's what the world needs—more of you!

There's MORE to you!

Michelle Washington

Hello Gorgeous,

You have been on my mind as I anticipate your new beginning. As you put on your shoes to walk into the next chapter of your life, I wanted to leave you with a love letter for you to read on your travels. On your life's journey you will experience people, places and things. This world can be cruel, and it can make you second guess who you are. When the world stares you in the face and tells you lies, boldly stand your ground and tell it to shut up. This world will have you believe that you are not good enough, and that you are not built for what is on the path before you. I am here to tell you that all of that is a lie. You are beyond capable of doing anything that you set your heart to. Trust me, it may not be easy, but it is possible. There may be detours along the way, but you will reach your destination.

Although the world can be cruel to us, we can be even harder on ourselves. I want you to remember that you are worthy of being the *you* that you were created to be; not a copycat of someone else. Being your true and authentic self comes with getting to know yourself personally. Be willing to spend time alone to reflect on your gifts, your talents, and even your adversities. Approach each day with intention. Set out to learn something new every day. Read books to feed your mind and expand your knowledge currency. Take your seat at the table and let your voice be heard; you have something to say. Surround yourself with girlfriends who are honest enough to tell you when you have lipstick on your teeth. Embrace the friends who will put a mirror up for you to see yourself and stand in your corner to encourage you. Keep the friends who will help you up when you fall.

My gorgeous friend; be unapologetically you! The unapologetic version of you doesn't get caught in the comparison trap. Unapologetically You is unapologetically unashamed of her. She embraces her strengths and her weaknesses. Unapologetically You is not afraid to fail. She wakes up every morning with a grateful heart.

Unapologetically You does not take life for granted. She looks herself in the mirror and crushes on the woman looking back at her. Unapologetically You takes care of herself so she can be her best self. She is #goals. Unapologetically You loves others even when they are unlovable. She is faithful to what is important to her. Unapologetically You lives her truth without regrets. She gives off a sweet aroma that cannot be bottled and reproduced. She wears the scent of her. Her unashamed self looks at her skin and sees the struggles of her ancestors. Without shame she looks at herself and sees a beautifully made woman.

So, when the world looks you in your face and says you are not who you know yourself to be, stand in the boldness of who you are, courageously show up in your authenticity, and be unapologetically unashamed.

Love you with my entire heart,

Kamela T. Smith

Dear Daughter,

My Beautiful Queen. Be you! I know life has tried to dispute the truth of who you are. You were born equipped and created to walk in a life that was wonderfully and purposely given to you. You are good; you are great; you are special; you are needed. What you offer the world has value. You are valuable. Remember that you are responsible for you. Stand firm on that. You are royalty; you are a Queen.

Being you will create your life story. Society and peers will work both intentionally and unintentionally to deter you from your life's purposed journey. Be you. Filter them out like weeds in a dead garden. No one can tell you how to be you, but you. You're an individual. We all are; therefore, it is also important that you understand and respect your peer's personal and purposed journey. Be wise, be strong, be beautiful, be unique—be you! When you're being you, you complete and compliment yourself. You matter. Never fear being you. Every part of you and your life is purposed, even though you may not fully understand it. Choose what guides, moves and leads you.

A great, healthy, strong, purposed life can only be fulfilled by being your unique self. The most important piece in your development is knowing that being who you are will grant you access into discovering your strengths and weaknesses. It is impossible to know this if you're living life as a fake version of you. In doing so, you will feel different, alone, and as if you don't belong. Choose what fills you up.

You are capable! Get excited, be inspired, have faith, be supportive, support yourself and praise yourself. Cheers! Cheer yourself. Toast! Toast yourself. Celebrate! Celebrate yourself. Fail! Fail for yourself. Failing gives you room to fail forward. Shine on, glow on, grow on, and go get your purpose on. Be grateful for who you are and who you were created to be. Don't allow others to mute you or make you tiptoe into a life that's not intended for you. Choose you, daily! Love you, daily! You are wonderful! You are awesome! Never allow anyone to program you into thinking you're "too much." This is a heavy phrase that normally confirms you're right on track. They'll attempt to persuade you into settling for less than who you are. You'll begin to feel trapped, stuck and unhappy, which will cause bitterness to enter and dwell within your temple.

I learned early on that no one could be me other than me. I had to stand on that and embrace it. Although it was many years ago, I can clearly hear my mother and other teachers I know chanting, "You're unique!" That stuck with me. When the crowds went left, I went right. I considered it a gift which existed within me that I didn't have to work hard on at all. I hope to gift this to you: the ability to go left when everyone else goes right, the strength to be you when it's uncomfortable, and the willingness to support others in being their authentic selves as you stand in the power of who you are. There is an indescribable satisfaction and sense of accomplishment that comes from being true to ourselves. That is what I desire for you. Be you, beautiful queen, be you!

All my love,

Brunette Kirtdoll Smith

Sweet Sister,

I know you've seen some difficult things in life and had to learn to swallow pain that cut and burned you. I want you to know I am sorry for the pain you endured. Suffering is not easy, especially when you have to go it alone. But what you need to know is that everything you experienced up to this point in your life has been preparing you to be someone great. Someone strong and more powerful than you could have been without those struggles.

You may never receive an apology from those who hurt you and you may never be able to make sense of your experiences. Still, I promise you this, the moment you choose to accept that there are things you can never change and practice releasing resentment and bitterness, you free yourself to be yourself. Learning to be your true, authentic self is perhaps the most pain-staking challenge you will face in your life. This is because we often give our joy and power away when we come across difficult situations. When that happens, we unconsciously try to protect ourselves by forming walls around our hearts so that no one can hurt us again. We don't realize it until too late that those walls might keep people from getting too close to us—but they also prevent us from living a full and loving life.

Baby girl, you've got to believe in yourself. This word *believe*, comes from the Latin word *beloved*. It states that to be yourself, you must love yourself. You can only do this if you let go of the lies you've told yourself about who you are and start loving every tender part of you. Hear me sister, you deserve to experience your own good love. That may feel hard to do, but you've got to be bigger than your beliefs. You have to know that holding on to those old wounds will keep you stuck and small; and worse, separated from love. Don't give your power away to foolish people who can't guide themselves, let alone guide you. It's time you take back your power. Once you decide to be yourself and not care what the voices in your head or anyone else has to say about who you are supposed to be, then you can live in the fullness of who you are created to be.

Sister, you were created to be magnificent. Wild. Extraordinary. Sometimes a bit outrageous. Always courageous and never, ever dull. You are the shine that sparkles when you speak. You are the light that attracts others when you walk into the room with full confidence in who you are. You have the power to help others remember to live more fully when you speak your truth from a place of love and not shame, blame, or as a victim.

You must believe in yourself. Until you can fully believe in who you are and what you're capable of, borrow from the belief I have in you. Read these words over and over again so you can feel my love coming through the pages. I am rooting for you. You and I may never meet, we may never get the chance to hug, but I believe in you and want to see you shine bigger than you could have ever imagined possible.

Love,

Veronica Lynn Clark

...Bold

Greetings to My Sister-Friend,

It has often been said that the Black woman's voice (your voice) is the moderating conscience of this American nation. As women, girls, sisters, daughters, aunties and mothers; society values us for carrying, birthing and raising future generations. At the same time though, you may be asked to forget about your own needs, cast aside your own goals, and suppress your own mind. You will be asked to speak comforting words in nurturing and supporting ways, even while you observe the undermining of your own communities of color. You might even one day be cautioned about creating a reputation of being the "angry Black woman." As Michel Martin, NPR host said, "Michelle Obama, Oprah and Serena Williams all have something in common. At some point during their public lives, they were labeled as angry." Note that all three are successful women in their own rights. Therefore, know that the title of angry Black woman is something you may also be called when using your voice to speak against those who might want to own your mind, manage you, or even manhandle you.

You might be called angry in the classroom when you disagree with a patriarchal interpretation of literary characters. Expect to be called angry if you speak up about the aggression of forces in your community trying to undermine the rights of your youth. Expect to be called angry if you speak up in the workplace about gender equity or equal pay for equal work. Expect to be called angry for taking a stand against microaggressions; and expect to be called an angry Black woman when you advocate for full rights of citizenship—be it to vote, live free from gun violence, or to be paid a living wage.

I wanted to tell you what you might encounter, so you will recognize it when it happens. More importantly though, I want you to know so you will do what it takes to manage it. I am writing to remind you that you are from a line of bold women who had voices and knew how to use them. You are surrounded by bold women who push bold agendas in both quiet and loud ways. Like Michelle, Oprah and Serena; bold women push, and they deliver in strategic ways. To be bold with your voice requires self-assurance and self-confidence. Know that you have it in you to build and develop both of these traits. If your life circumstances do not give you the people who will cultivate and reaffirm these traits in you, make it a personal goal to seek people who will. If you have already mastered these traits, then use your voice to embolden your sisters in the village.

Know that self-assurance and self-confidence will come from you having self-knowledge. That knowledge of who you are must be a primary pursuit. Know that your history is full of women who became self-assured and self-confident by knowing their own value, clarifying their own interests, mastering their own skills, and commanding their abilities for good.

You, like all of us as women, were born with a voice. However, not all of us learn to use ours effectively in service of the village. You have it in you to build the traits that will allow you to lean into any name calling, stand up for what you believe, and carry forward a bold agenda for your life. So be bold, sister-friend. Be bold!

Love,

Dr. Marcia F. Robinson

Dear Sister,

Be is to *exist. Bold* is a descriptor of how you can choose to exist or show up in the world with confidence and courage. Be bold. Two very subtle, yet powerful words. When put together they are a command! The idea that you have the ability to be bold may be exciting, however knowing that you must be bold can be overwhelming and daunting.

Let's talk a bit about superheroes. Superheroes are characters with special abilities. Whether they were born with such abilities or they trained and earned their abilities, they have a unique skill designed for a particular situation. Through trial and error, they may have uncovered and developed these skills and abilities. Many times, they didn't even know they had what it took to resolve a situation until the situation presented itself. But when facing the issue, their unique skill and abilities shine and come forth. Once they have uncovered their superpower, it becomes easier and easier to use. The interesting thing about superheroes is that they don't win all the time! Sometimes they lose, but their unique skill and ability is not in question. They take the defeat and return stronger, better, and more prepared.

Beauty, there will undoubtedly be (if it hasn't happened already) times in your life when you will have to muster the energy to be bold and show an ability to take risks and be courageous. Life situations, relationships, and experiences will chip at your ability and desire to be bold. There will be situations you encounter that make you wonder if you should use your voice and walk in such confidence. To that, I'll say you have two of the most powerful tools that allow you to be bold; your presence and your voice. Your presence allows you to exist and show up. To be. Sis, if you are in a situation emotionally, spiritually or physically, then you have what it takes to enact boldness. Your voice gives words to your soul, your feelings, and your emotions. Use your voice to advocate for yourself, to give insight, and share your opinions. This is boldness. There will be times when your presence and voice are challenged. There may be a space or rooms where you feel your presence or voice will not be heard. To that I say—don't believe what you see, believe what you know. Trust your superpowers! If you are in that space or room, then you belong there, and you have something to contribute. Enact the energy and courage it will take to be a part of the action.

Darling, you are a superhero with superpowers! Be bold! Uncover your superpower. Use your presence and your voice. Show up and show out! No superhero shows up to a situation they know they are prepared to defeat, but then freezes, or doesn't address the issue! Instead, they arrive with the confidence of knowing they have what it takes and gives it their best; and if they don't win, that doesn't negate their ability or the pureness of their superpower. They will continue to show up again and again. They have confidence in knowing who they are, and whose they are. So, my love, live boldly, be bold. This is a command. "Be strong and very courageous" (Joshua 1:7 NIV).

You are loved,

Corinne M. Green

To My Unstoppable Sista,

I'm not surprised by your accomplishments; you've always had a heart to do what's right and create your very own lane. If I've never told you before, know that I value you. You were never afraid to be who you are, and now you are a force to be reckoned with. You never compromise or conform to the opinions or beliefs of others about you. I appreciate that about you and admire your courage to be yourself while choosing to be unnoticed on purpose. You are able to walk in a room and shift the entire atmosphere to light. You are able to look in the mirror and see uniqueness, beauty, and intellect and own it without boasting or bragging; that is a gift. You never seek to outshine others around you, although they have no problems doing so to you. You are adventurous and brilliant, and one of the women I admire most. You have the strength of a superhero; they too have weaknesses but never let those weaknesses stop them from using their power. You also demonstrate a phenomenal power of celebrating self and others. Thank you for the respect you've always had for yourself and other women. Thank you for encouraging and empowering women who thought of themselves as less than; you handled them with care, showing them that their power and purpose can pulverize any obstacle.

Look back over your life. Can you remember where you began? The odds were stacked against you. Statistically, you were to fall into government assistance, public housing, and be a high-school dropout. Ha; look at you now! You didn't allow your circumstances to dictate your path. Your attitude about life has always been victor and not victim; you were determined to make a difference! Not only for yourself, but for the lives of others. I'm sure you never imagined the gifts inside of you stored up, waiting to pour out and empower others once you stepped out of the naysayers' shadows. Yes, honey! I wonder if you knew you were created for greatness. You were purposed to be on this earth to impact everyone you come in contact with, despite how your story began. Most would have never overcome the obstacles you so elegantly maneuvered through. Celebrate all the things you survived that were meant to break you.

Although the encouragement of others came few and far between, you found an inner power that inspired you to keep going because you knew you would one day make a difference. Others secretly laughed at you; but their laughter was a cover for the intimidation they felt because of your assertiveness and vociferous opinion. You knew their assignment, yet you walked in grace and love. You knew they needed to experience their own healing to appreciate you. Your fierce attitude makes you unconquerable, brave, and confident; not caring how others perceive you. You've lived with the weight of the world on your shoulder, yet you carried it with grace. You never back down to what others see as a challenge, but fearlessly rise to the occasion. Sista, continue to be who you are; be bold!

Always rooting for you,

Tanisha L. Scott

Dear Beautiful Black Woman,

Growing up is scary; you have no idea what to expect, and you might be afraid to take those next steps. What now? I want to tell you, be bold! There is absolutely no reason to be afraid if you take it one step and one day at a time. Be confident; you are phenomenal, with the strength of a lion and wings of eagles. You will never know what you can accomplish if you do not try.

Remember, you are not on this journey alone; so many others have gone before you and are waiting to guide you, to hold your hand when needed, lend a shoulder to cry on, and laugh with you.

My dear sister, don't you know you were awesomely and wonderfully made? You are unique, the only you in the world. You may be light, brown or dark-skinned, but your natural tan is envied the world over. Have you looked in the mirror lately my dear? Take a second look at your sculptured features. The white in your eyes glistens. Your Nubian nose and pouting lips are characteristics to be proud of. Love the waistline that highlights your magnificent body. Hold your head high, with grace and confidence; you are God's masterpiece.

You, my dear, are a magnificent creation and a beautiful queen. No matter what you've had to overcome in life, it has prepared you for this day. You can walk fearlessly with strength and boldness, knowing that whatever lies ahead is not too daunting for you.

Don't be afraid to get out of your comfort zone. Try something new, meet new people, experience different cultures. You will be amazed at the tremendous growth and life skills you will gain. Believe and trust in the power that is greater than you. You were created by God for a purpose; trust that He will guide you to and through whatever may come.

Have you ever wondered why you are here? It was not a mistake—your existence was planned by a higher power. Please know that all things will work out according to your specific plan because you are called to a bright future. Surrender to the call to be more than you think you can be. When you think you've given life your all, reach down deep inside and give more and watch doors open for you.

Be bold and courageous dear sister; that's how you will reach your true potential. Live your truth. How will you ever know what you are capable of if you live in fear? It's been said that fear is "False Evidence Appearing Real." Fear cannot define you; stand up and stare it down. Change your perspective. I say fear is "Face Everything And Rise!"

Look at yourself in the mirror every day, choose to believe the best about you, and affirm yourself with positive words. Choose to live a life of favor. Choose to walk in the power of the One who created you. Stand tall, hold your head up, keep your back straight, smile, and be bold. Be confident in who you are. I believe in you.

With much love and blessings,

Candia Cumberbatch-Lucenius

To My Beautiful Black Girls,

I often feel relieved knowing you get to experience things differently than I did growing up. There were so many times in my life where I struggled to be in my body. I burned my scalp multiple times straightening my hair so it wouldn't be nappy (I didn't know better). I wore concealers that didn't match my shade. I never embraced my quirks. I am discovering my own fashion style at 38; and in my teenage years, I would have rather tried to make my way blindly than wear my glasses. I struggled a lot growing up, and I hope to be here for you to make those times easier. You have an amazing opportunity to grow up with confidence. You, my sweet girl, live in a time where kinks and coils give you character. Makeup is produced in hundreds of shades (thank you, Rihanna). Your dark skin is desired by many, and to be Black and proud is a way of life, not a social movement.

It is in this space, at this moment, that you should be bold in your existence. Far too often I see beautiful brown-skin girls walking with their head down, not embracing the fact that they are the descendants of queens. As a community, we have forgotten to speak life into our sweet little girls; and for that, I apologize. We must do better, because I genuinely believe if you knew you were royalty, then you would act with absolute confidence. So, let's erase any doubts.

Each piece of your body is special. Your walk, your laugh, your smile, your eyes, your legs, your belly, your elbows, your knees and every little jiggle makes this world a better place. There is literally no one else on this earth who is the same in every way as you. Your mere existence makes the sun shine brighter. Your contribution to the world is so significant we can't put a value on it. Your femininity is empowering. Your strength is inspiring, and your courage is humbling.

You, my darling, have a purpose. You were not created by accident. You are not a mistake. You are not a burden, and even if you can't see it, someone is smiling because you are here (wild guess—it's me). You deserve to be treated with respect, and you deserve all the love your heart can hold. You deserve to cry tears of happiness, experience moments of joy, and experience failure surrounded by so much love that you'll never feel you have fallen too far to get back up again. Your confidence is contagious, and you have the opportunity to be the spark that lights a fire in the world. I don't know how many times you will read this, but I pray that each time you do there is a part of you that redefines herself knowing that you are destined for greatness. Your skin does not define who you are, but it gives you access to generations of phenomenal women, so you can stand on their shoulders to reach your dream. I hope one day you consider me one of those women. Chin up, Princess! Walk boldly into your future.

Love,

Dr. Jessica A. Spradley

Hey Rockstar!

Life has sure served you a few blows, huh? Like you, I've been knocked down more times than I can count. There were times I struggled to get up and there were a lot of times I wanted to stay down. I didn't think I had the strength to get up again. Those blows hurt, and each one was more intense than the last. The damage done was more internal than external. Meaning, I mastered covering up the physical bruises with my smile, makeup, and hair, and I excelled professionally; but those mental and emotional bruises had me bleeding internally. The more I seemed to win publicly, the more I was dying inside.

Life has a way of being a bully, taking over our lives and making us respond to its shenanigans, rather than living our dreams. It's easy to lose sight of what we really want to do when we are constantly reminded of our past hurts, traumas, and failures. Those issues make our environment toxic and harder for us to breathe. Like me, you may have considered not trying again. Don't make any waves; keep your head low, and just do what it takes to get by. However, your dreams haunt you and are constant reminders of the power and purpose inside of you. Do you dare try again? Do you dare push past the nightmares of your past and the hardships of your current dilemmas to embrace unknown treasures of your future? Dear sis, yes! Run, walk, crawl, or roll towards that finish line! You are so worth it and more than capable of achieving it! Listen to me; look at the calendar and document the date. Now, look in the mirror and say "hi" to yourself! I want you to realize you've physically survived your past. Do the necessary work to mentally and emotionally free yourself so you can activate your power and conquer your current obstacles. You can do it. Other people may have counted you out. Other people may have mishandled you; don't you mishandle you.

Consider your past a boot camp for your future. It's all been preparation for this moment in your life. Whatever you desire is available if you are bold enough to pursue it. The audacity of life to hurt you. The audacity of others to mishandle you. The audacity of people to not see your value. Now consider the audacity of you, to live out your wildest dreams while the world watches in amazement! They'll whisper; they'll try to bring up your past failures. They'll try to distract you; you'll consider quitting. Don't shrink, sis! Take a deep breath, look yourself in the mirror, and remember you are not what happened to you. You are and have always been more than enough! You possess world-changing capabilities! The world—including the naysayers—need you to fulfill your purpose! They need to know that it's possible. When you dare to walk fiercely in your purpose, you give them hope that it's possible for them as well. Consider the idea that you don't have to deal with life; life has to deal with you!

Be bold, sis; you are a force to be reckoned with! Dry your tears, world-changer; you are the phenomenon the world has been waiting for! You've been hiding in plain sight. Do the necessary work to free yourself emotionally and mentally of your fears and inhibitions. Look yourself in the mirror and laugh out loud. They never considered the audacity of you to win!

Love,

Shirelle Diamond Hogans

...Vulnerable

To My Beautiful Daughters,

Vulnerability is uncomfortable, unnerving and undesirable, but it is an inevitable and necessary part of life. You may think being vulnerable means you are weak. You might believe that if you are vulnerable, people will take advantage of you. You may be afraid that being vulnerable requires you to give up control and face shame. If this is how you think, I'm sure you're wondering why anyone would ever want to be vulnerable. Here's the truth: vulnerability leads to liberation, happiness, and personal growth.

Contrary to popular belief, it is okay to be vulnerable. In fact, it is often required to get what you need or want. Never let the fear of vulnerability rob you of relationships, opportunity, and the joy of life. You often build stronger relationships, rather than destroy them, when you are vulnerable. Sharing your truth, thoughts, and feelings with others creates comfort, safety, and trust. You learn to love and be loved; you learn to be open and accept openness, and you learn to connect with others on a deeper level without fear or regret.

Being your authentic, vulnerable self opens doors to opportunity. When you discover and embrace your flaws, they work for you not against you. Your flaws and quirks are the very things that make you unique and special. When you stand out, others will take notice. When the opportunity presents itself, be vulnerable enough to take the risk and believe in the impossible.

Being vulnerable gives you peace, and peace gives you joy. No human being is perfect. Chasing perfection leads to anxiety, procrastination, and unhappiness. Be courageous and vulnerable enough to let down your guard, accept what you can't change, let go of hurt, forgive and love. When you can do this, you can experience life more fully.

Being vulnerable allows you to learn and grow through openness and honesty. It allows you to be true to yourself and others around you. Being vulnerable gives others a glimpse of your heart, and a peek into your soul. Your willingness to be vulnerable gives others permission to be vulnerable and empathetic. Vulnerability is a coming together of strength, courage, power and love. This gift exists inside of you. It's time to open it up.

Love,

Dr. Charlotte Brickhouse

Dear Little Black Girl,

There will be choices. I rise every morning tired, in need of more sleep, restless, anxious and immediately feeling the pressure of the choices I have to make for the day. My life as a Black woman is not without burden; it is not weightless. The honor and power I hold as a Black woman does not allow me to escape this weight, not even for a moment. It is a cold, bitter, confusing world in which you will constantly be placed in situations where you feel you have to choose. Choose sides. Choose beliefs. Choose values. Choose paths. Choose the best option. Choose the right option. Choose wisely.

Some choices feel clear and right, while others may feel complex and confusing. Some choices feel impossible to make. Some choices will be a matter of life or death. Then there are those choices where the line between right and wrong is a blur. Where you see the validity in both sides. Where you could argue a good case either way and feel convicted by either outcome. Where compromise still feels like you are letting someone down and where the world seemingly would be a better place with either choice. No clear right answer; yet a choice must be made.

Oh, Black woman! I want to tell you that in those all too common moments where a choice is desired, needed and warranted—when you know the consequences of each choice and neither is acceptable; where the thought of someone losing and another winning causes you to pause; and when the decision is presented as an either/or option—not choosing is okay. Waiting, listening and keeping still until you receive a pull from the universe is okay.

There is no single step that comes before a choice. There are more conversations to be had, more ideas to be shared, more scenarios to play out, and always more information to be found. The fact that a choice has to be made should not be the only reason you make a choice. What I've learned is that not making a choice, not deciding, not choosing to conform to the dualities often presented, and not choosing the lesser of two evils, is often the better choice.

Shifting the conversation from *either/or* to *both/and* will require you to be vulnerable; to be open, emotionally raw, honest with yourself and with your community. Search your heart for what really matters; what you care about. Consider that all of your cares can be equal; one does not have to supersede the other. Be vulnerable; be ready to confess the things you don't know and don't understand as much as those things of which you're not sure. Be okay with not having the answers; and be okay with seeking them.

Regardless how heavy things may feel some mornings, I also wake up hopeful, energized, and excited in anticipation of what our future holds with you leading us; with you empowered to make choices that serve the greater good. My greatest hope is that you will take the lead and show others how to be vulnerable, so we can make choices to improve our future.

Love,

Melissa Johnson Hewitt

Dear Black Girl,

I am writing this letter not only to you, but also to Black women who still wrestle with the hurt experienced as a Black girl that you thought was tucked away or buried. Someone recently posed this question to me, "Based on all your life experiences and knowing all that you know now, what advice would you share with your 10-year-old self?" My response was simply, "Be vulnerable." Being vulnerable means having the courage to be imperfect and using your voice to speak your truth. Baby girl; don't let anyone stifle your voice, not even your parents. My father wanted my life to be so much better than his that he could not hear or see me. He corrected and criticized everything I did or said that did not align with the life he wanted for me. In hindsight, I'm sure he was demonstrating his love and desires for me the best way he knew how, but it made me feel like I was not enough in his eyes. I allowed that experience to silence my voice and I acted out in anger towards men for decades. I made sure that I did everything perfectly (or so I thought) so no one could question how I showed up in the world. I allowed one person to silence the authentic voice that my God gave me to share with the world.

The world sees vulnerability as the core of shame, fear, and a struggle for worthiness and belonging. You may wonder why I am asking you to appear weak when you know deep in your heart that you are smarter than anyone in your class, that your God gives you the strength to do all things, and that your life experiences have prepared you to be one step ahead of your peers. We have a tendency to accept the world's definition of a word rather than exploring the full meaning of it. Let me clarify what vulnerability really is. Vulnerability is the birthplace of joy, creativity, belonging and love. I did not find that out until I was 45 years old; after I graduated high school and college, after my parents divorced, after I lost my mother tragically, after many failed relationships, and after I left my legal career. I don't want you to experience the same delay in understanding and experiencing the power of vulnerability.

Your vulnerability is what makes you beautiful. Vulnerability is not comfortable, but it is necessary to open your heart and find your authentic voice, especially after you have allowed someone else to silence it. To be vulnerable is to stop controlling and predicting life and live in the present moment open to whatever lesson there is to learn from each experience as it comes. The world silences vulnerability; but Black girl, remember this—you can't silence the hurt without silencing your emotions. When you silence the hurt, you cut off joy, you disable gratitude, you eliminate happiness, and you close the door to your heart.

Let yourself be seen—deeply seen, vulnerably seen, to love with your whole heart by using your voice. Believe that you are enough! Because when you work from a place where you believe you are enough, no one can silence your voice. When you have the courage to be imperfect, you are unstoppable!

I love you! I see you! I hear you!

Your sister forever,

Heather D. Horton

My Dear Sister,

Learn how to be okay with the scars, disappointments, misunderstandings, missteps, and mistakes you've experienced in life. Scars are reminders that a traumatic event happened here. They are like a tag left on your soul. A tag is an identifying mark, or something left behind without any real connection or thought.

These words, without any real connection, expose the soul of a sister and this is where vulnerability comes in. In that very moment of your consciousness, you (your soul) have a decision to make about that scar (that tag). You decide whether you will be embarrassed by the scar. You decide if you will look for opportunities to hide your scar, or whether you just let the scar heal. Will you let the scar breathe by leaving it exposed to fresh air (perspective) or will you put a band-aid on it? Band-aids have the potential to extend a wound's healing time; especially when they are used to cover the ugliness of the scar rather than as a protective covering during dangerous situations. What a huge difference it is to have a bandage that is a cover up versus a bandage that covers up. Will you care for your scar by watching it, cleaning it, and nursing it? The decision is yours.

Cover your scars my sister, to protect your healing; but be sensitive to when you must remove the bandage so that your wounds can breathe. Protect your scars from potential exposure to toxic things. If your wound is exposed to toxicity for extended periods of time, you will find that the wound morphs into more of a stripe—a deeply impacted wound that cuts through flesh. Pay attention to how you heal. Watch for the possibility of re-injury. Look for the scales of your scar to dry as they prepare to fall off. The scab of the scar will fall naturally, if you allow.

Sister, life will present opportunities for you to process the points of trauma as either a stripe or a scar. Life will happen. Life consists of ebbs and flows. You may have to pause and go in a different direction. You may have to wait or struggle through to the finish line, doing all of this as someone else is watching. Trust your instinct to know the difference between taking a break, staying the course, and redirecting your energy. Each action requires faith. Each action has the potential to expose your scars (vulnerabilities). You will not be the first one to experience this scar, and you won't be the last, so embrace your scar and keep advancing your purpose.

Vulnerability can cause you to feel alone and unsure. Be encouraged by the promises of God that are alive in you. These promises speak to the soul, even the ones that bear scars. Speak to your conscious soul, recall every promise to your mind and have hope. "The Lord will guide you continually giving you water when you are dry and restoring your strength. You will be like a well-watered garden, like an ever-flowing spring" (Isaiah 58:11 NLT). With these promises, your vulnerability will settle in its proper perspective and in its proper space. With these promises, your vulnerability does not have to tag you with no real connection. With these promises, you can be healed, and you can be protected.

Sincerely,

Jeri Johnson

Beautiful Black Girls,

Your skin tones, curls, kinks and coils—the simplicity of your existence adds a beautiful complexity to this world. The world is a better place because of the authentic traits you have yet to awaken inside of you! I am proud of you, and I anticipate the full blossoming of your being. In a world that has yet to accept and honor your vulnerability, I want to encourage you to be vulnerable, anyway.

Beautiful Black Girl, I refuse to lie to you. Life will be hard, and it will hurt at times. You will laugh, grow and evolve, but you will also cry, sweat and bleed. No matter the circumstances, know that in time you will always come out better and wiser. Why? Because you chose to live through it. Do you know what happens when you live through everything life throws your way?

I want you to envision your favorite luxury car; your dream car, to be exact. Got it in your head? Great! Now, put on your favorite designer clothes, shoes, and shades, and picture yourself sitting in the driver's seat at the intersection of two roads. Both roads lead to the same destination. The first road is paved beautifully. There are hills, curves and sharp turns that you can't see. You don't have to worry though; there is ample space and lighting for you to drive with no problems and arrive at your destination without damage to your car. The second road is unpaved; in fact, it's very uneven, bumpy, and has tall grass, weeds, fallen trees and branches all over. You can drive through it, but you will have to be careful not to damage your car or hurt yourself as you go forward. So, you have two options in front of you; which road will you choose? Most will choose the road that is already paved—the road clear of harmful objects and debris. That's the smart choice.

Do you know that, when you experience the trials and tribulations of life and forgive and heal from the treacherous terrain you conquered, you create a beautiful paved road for the next brown girl to travel? You become evidence—a living demonstration—that she too can make it through to the other side. Vulnerability connects you to our global sisterhood. When you share your story of hardship, healing and strength, it ignites passion, drive, and purpose in those you share it with. You now become a contagious beacon of hope and inspiration to other girls and women who look like you. Your transparency and honesty about things that could have derailed you, stopped you, or even killed you do not expose your weaknesses. They demonstrate your strength. Black girl, you are strong because you remain vulnerable. Never lose that attribute and never tire of sharing your experiences. You may have traveled that road alone, but you are now equipped to help another sister on her journey. We need you, sis. We need your story. We need to know your journey so we can create a beautifully paved road for those who will follow us. So please, Black Girl, be vulnerable.

Following in your footsteps,

Meagan Ferrare

...Fearless

Listen Sis,

You are fearlessly made. Starting today you will no longer hide behind the talents and gifts you were given. Sometimes the mind can play foolish games with you to disturb your peace and block your vision. Do not allow this to happen! There is only one you. We are bombarded with images in the media of what we should be, how we should act and even how we should dress. But I'm here to tell you, that is not your journey. In fact, you are a class act all on your own. It is not meant for everyone to understand your journey. I know you're uneasy about your hesitation. What are you thinking? You're not good enough? You don't have enough money to start that business? You'll wait until the kids get older? Maybe you've tried before, and it wasn't a success.

This was not a failure; it was a setup for better opportunities. Now you know exactly what it takes to succeed as you move forward. Set yourself up with other like-minded women who share the same goals as you. Keep your sister-girl circle tight. What! You don't know what a sister-girl circle is? Your sister-girl circle is a group of women who will cheer you on. When you get off track, they will politely, with no hesitation, direct you back to your goals. They will support your business endeavors, whether it means purchasing a product or helping with marketing by word of mouth. See, the resources and support you need are there, but guess what? It all starts with you.

If you are waiting for perfection, it will never happen. Embrace imperfect starts. Some of the best success stories come from mistakes. You will never truly be happy until you live in your truth. So, what is next? Well, start writing what you would like to see happen in the next few months. Seriously, write this down. Start with small goals that will not cause you anxiety but will hold you accountable. As you accomplish these goals, pay attention to how your mood changes. You'll become more confident. You'll feel a sense of accomplishment. Nothing can get in your way. Now mind you, this doesn't mean you will not run into roadblocks. The idea is to remain on track and not give up. Turn your dreams into action plans and execute them. Give yourself reasonable deadlines. Don't sit on this any longer. You've waited too long; this is your time to shine. Don't let another minute or another second go by without moving forward to complete this vision. I'm telling you, if you wait too long you will be right back where you started. This is not to discourage you, but to tell you the truth. Be vigilant in this pursuit.

Sis, I'm so proud of you. You will reach unimaginable heights if you remain focused. Just don't forget, you are wonderfully and fearfully made. Be fearlessly you! Don't be afraid to be bold and fearless! I'm telling you; this is your year to shine. You will no longer hide in the fear that will stop you from greatness. What are you waiting for?

Your sister,

Alicia R. Acklin

My Beloved,

When I was a girl, my mother told me I could do or be anything I wanted. She always believed in me, even when I didn't believe in myself. Because she was my biggest cheerleader, it helped me step out on faith and imagine the possibilities. The power of faith can never be underestimated. I've been a witness and know in my core it is real. Any setbacks experienced; every fear encountered; I turned to my foundation of faith. No matter what the challenge, I trusted in God. When self-doubt reared its ugly head, that's where I turned and grew in confidence.

Beloved, I want for you what was given to me—the gift of encouragement. When you are silenced, speak up and use your voice. When you face the unknown, stand boldly. When told that you cannot, know that you are capable. I am your supporter. I am planting the seed of faith, showing you that fear will not stop the show; keeping you focused on your dreams. Now is your time; stand firm and dream the impossible. I'm pushing you. I'm whispering in your ear, "Go for it! Fight fear! Focus on faith!"

Fear disguised as self-doubt can rob potential. Complacency steps in and if allowed, will take over. Step up and watch God show out. Get busy. Set and focus on your goals. Greatness can be realized if you do your part. We're coming together as friends, mothers, grandmothers, aunts, and sisters, to encourage you to know that you can dream the unimaginable. Beloved, you are our future. We will be role models and set positive examples. We know you are watching and listening. Because of this, we must lead by example—following in the footsteps of the faith-fueled, the faith-full and the faithful who came before us; Bessie Coleman, Madame C.J. Walker, Shirley Chisholm, and Michelle Obama.

Beloved, my journey is a lesson I pass to you; my testimony of how fear collided with faith and the latter was victorious. In May 2009, I was negatively affected by the economy and downsized from a rewarding job of nine years. The day before the news came, I had an eerie feeling my name would be called and I would lose my job. As I prepared to go to church, I listened to an evangelist speak to his congregation about stretching one's faith. His words spoke to me. In contemplation, I was complacent, unmotivated, unhappy and fearful. I allowed fear to keep me there, and it won. After being downsized, I had to step back and recall all the things I learned from my mother; what she taught me about fear and facing it. Her lessons resonated with me. I knew I had to get busy, do my part and step up so that God would show up—and boy did He ever. I stretched my faith, and through much prayer, God had a plan for me. He closed one door and opened another. My faith gave me the courage and confidence to leave everything I was used to and take a job in Japan.

Beloved, like those mentioned who paved the way by opening doors, I will pave the way each day for you. I will continue to teach you to face fear head-on with boldness and confidence. You must believe in yourself as I believe in you. We may not know what tomorrow brings, but I know that with faith you can face it with success.

With love,

Tonya L. Horn

Fearless Lady,

Be fearless, girl! Fear is an unpleasant emotion caused by the belief that someone or something is dangerous and likely to cause pain or a threat. Fear is also an amazing power. It encourages us to survive. It's also a restricting mental block that can keep you from accomplishing your goals. Fear makes room for lame reasons to creep in and control you. Don't allow fear to do what it does best in your life, which is limit you. Understand you will be nervous, vulnerable, and afraid at times—but never allow these things to control your everyday life. Remember that fear is an emotion; and it is mind over matter.

Once you make the conscious decision to just do what you have to do, fear can no longer limit you from anything. When you break the barriers of fear, you have then unlocked what has been placed inside of you. The doctor who wants to save people's lives and cure sicknesses has been released. The writer and poet who has a story ready to write has been released. The first female president has been released. The singer/songwriter is released. All the talents you have inside you come to life because you did not allow fear to dictate your decisions.

Embrace every journey God is taking you on because He created you to be set apart. Understand that your purpose is intriguing and can change people's lives. Know that you can accomplish all of your goals when you operate through faith. When you believe in yourself and your purpose, you can no longer be ruled by fear because you have become fearless. Know that when you have a determined mindset that nothing becomes impossible to you. The sky is not the limit. You keep going and achieving everything you want. Imagine getting up in the morning, putting on battle armor, and everything you walk through gets knocked down. The armor is your determination and what you knock down are things that try to stop you from accomplishing your goals. When you strap yourself with the mindset of determination, nothing impedes your purpose and calling. Tell yourself, "I will fight through the fear and I will achieve all of my goals because I can." So, remember to be fearless because your purpose needs you. Be fearless so the next girl ready to stand up and achieve her goals can look to you for motivation. Be fearless so the next generation can see there was someone like them once before. You are fearless, so be fearless!

Love,

Elon Jeffcoat

Dear African Princess,

As you go through life, you will learn many lessons along the way. One of the first lessons you will learn is that life is not always fair. People are not always fair. Injustice and mistreatment are a common problem that many of us often face. In life, you will face many challenges and obstacles. You must be strong enough to overcome those obstacles and not let the obstacles overcome you.

Never be afraid to stand up for yourself, to stand up for justice and to stand up for what you believe. It is not always comfortable to speak out against a situation that is unfair; even if it's a situation that others have accepted as normal. I want you to realize that incorrect and unfair behavior can often become an accepted way of life after it's been allowed to continue for a long period of time. Slavery was a way of life in this country for hundreds of years, but that didn't make it right. The people who fought against slavery were brave and fearless. They helped bring about a change that benefited every slave in this country. It changed the course of our nation. It was a difficult fight. It didn't come without a cost. You must have the same courage when you stand up for yourself against any injustice you face in life.

Be fearless and challenge any oppressive situation. If it affects you, it either has or will affect someone else. Change will not and does not occur unless the unjust situation or person is confronted and challenged. Just realize that some people will resist change. They may resist and resent you; they may try to scandalize your name or hurt you in other ways. Don't lose hope; just remember that anything worth having is worth fighting for. My mother used to tell me that if you don't stand up for something, you'll fall for anything. So, stand up, be bold, and be fearless; however, know that you will sometimes have to stand alone. Others may be afraid to speak out. They may fear the repercussions. Don't be afraid to be the person who brings about a positive change. Your fearlessness may change not only your life, but also the lives of many others. Change doesn't come about by being quiet, it comes about when someone becomes frustrated enough to speak up and take action.

Fear is paralyzing. When a person is paralyzed, he or she is unable to move or take any action. You are too strong and beautiful to allow fear to paralyze you. Believe in yourself, believe in your cause, and be courageous enough to stand up for it. Courage is the ability to face your fears, despite the dangers. When I think of you, I am reminded of a beautiful African princess, ready to courageously face the challenges this life offers and ready to make a positive impact in this world.

Love,

Malinda Bova

My Dearest Sister,

I know how the troubles of life can seem to come out of nowhere. One minute you're thanking God for your home, your significant other or your job; the next moment, what feels like tragedy strikes and knocks the wind out of you. I know that you sometimes go from complete happiness and confidence to despair and confusion. You ask yourself why these things always seem to happen to you. Why can't the universe just let you be happy? I know my sister, because I've asked myself the same questions.

I also know that because of those situations you've closed yourself off from family, friends, potential mates and even from life. You're afraid, and that's natural. It's natural to protect yourself. But let me ask you this; do you know yourself anymore, sister? Stop and ask yourself that question. Take your time and think. Do you know who you are and what you're capable of achieving, or have you let fear consume and transform you into someone God never intended? Are you meek and pensive, or defensive and guarded? Are you in the same situation this year as you were last year? If the answer is yes, I want you to understand that it's all rooted in fear. You see, the funny thing about fear, my sister, is that even though it's natural and sometimes necessary, it can seep into every aspect of your life, transform the way you view the world, and eventually the way you view yourself, if you let it.

We are taught that being afraid means that we are weak, so we ignore it or attempt to hide it. But on the contrary, being afraid simply means that we are human. While fear is a normal part of our flesh, understand that it is often an illusion; a trick and a mind game meant to stunt our personal growth, block our blessings, and keep us stagnant year after year. The way we respond to fear makes all the difference. We can't control the ups and downs of life, nor can we control other people's actions. However, what we can control is our response to the inevitable fears that we experience.

What you thought was a tragedy from your childhood, relationships or perceived failures was actually a springboard to your highest self. So, I challenge you to respond courageously with defiance and unwavering determination against the fear. Don't shamefully ignore it because that allows fear to grow. Instead, look fear directly in the eyes and declare out loud, "I may be afraid, but I am courageous! I can do hard things! I am becoming the best possible version of myself!" I believe in you, my sister. Believe in yourself; and when you can't, stand on my shoulders and the shoulders of the courageous women who support you until you believe in your heart and soul, "I am courage personified!"

Love,

Nisa K. Williams

To My Sisters,

Do you know what it looks like to be fearless? Maybe it looks like confronting your abuser or forgiving their transgressions and releasing them from your thought life. Maybe it looks like leaving a loveless marriage or staying in it because of the children. Maybe it looks like quitting your 9 to 5 so you can continue your education or going back to school despite your 9 to 5. Maybe it looks like saying no to a friend who is taking more than they are giving, going against the grain in the way you parent despite what the parent magazines encourage, or walking away from the faith you were raised to believe in even though your entire family still believes in it. Maybe it looks like selling everything you own to live life off the grid or investing your life savings in an apartment building. Maybe it looks like being a passive member of society, living a peaceful and sedentary life amid all the political, economic and environmental chaos, joining no movement, signing not one petition, or passing on your right to vote.

Being fearless, my sister, does not mean the absence of fear. I believe being fearless means giving fear less space in our lives, in our minds and in our hearts, to accomplish what we set out to do, to be who we desire to be, and to live out what we believe in; regardless of the unknown, even when we're unsure of the outcome or consequence of a decision made. You do it anyway, because you believe it is the right thing for you to do in your life.

No doubt this can be a tricky road to travel. As with almost everything in life, there is a caveat to this thing called fearlessness, because being fearless can look selfish and reckless. I have a saying: Do you and do no harm. Being fearless does not mean the reckless abandonment of basic human principles like love and kindness. So, I encourage you to seek counsel from others who may have "been there and done that" regarding a decision you are trying to make that may affect the lives of others. Your power, your being fearless, is by no means diminished. You are being wise, and you are being smart.

Be fearless my sister, in whatever way that looks to you. You have been uniquely created to live this life in a way that only you can. So, whatever you do, do it fearlessly. Whoever you decide to become—be her, fearlessly. Whatever you decide to believe in—believe it, fearlessly.

Your fearless sister,

C. Wilkinson Davis

...A Light

Dear Beautiful Beloved Sister,

The presence of the divine finds its unique expression in you and calls for the light within you to emanate. You are a life-giving and nourishing force for good in the universe. The light within you twinkles when you smile and flashes when you laugh. It is a laser that penetrates the deep hurt of a broken world when you extend compassion and forgiveness. Let your light shine!

We live in a very imperfect world with imperfect, broken people. It is a world where we will all encounter hurt in some form or another. Whether it is disappointment, failure, rejection, loss, abandonment, sadness, or even malice and hate; none of us escape this earth without being touched by its brokenness. Darkness, however, cannot consume light. Darkness can only attempt to obstruct and conceal light, to diminish it. Light penetrates darkness and where it is present, it will find any crack or crevice to shine through. Allow your inner light to fuel your soul, and ignite a fire where the flames of love, peace, joy and purpose burn bright; where others find the warmth of kindness, humility, and acceptance in your glow.

In each encounter and every endeavor, there is always a choice—your choice. Will you cast a shadow of tepid darkness that harbors the moldy spores of bitterness and apathy? Choose instead to give way to light that enriches the soil where goodness grows, healing is cultivated, and life thrives!

Be a light! Whether you shimmer, twinkle, sparkle, glow, glimmer, glisten, flicker or flash; allow goodness to radiate from within you.

Light always attracts light! Burn bright, and don't allow anyone or anything to steal your shine!

Shine bright my sister,

Lois T. Miller

Hello, My Beautiful Daughter!

I want you to close your eyes for a second and sing with me, "This little light of mine, I'm gonna let it shine! This little light of mine! I'm gonna let it shine! This little light of mine. I'm gonna let it shine. Let it shine. Let it shine. Let it shine!" Ah! Doesn't that feel good? I want you to remember this feeling. Remember how good it feels down in your soul when you let your light shine. Your light is like a beautiful hug from God designed especially for you. Your light is your inner glow which beams all the way from the top of your gorgeous head to your darling toes. When you smile, you radiate your light. Keep smiling and shining my beautiful daughter; your smile lights up the world.

When you shine your light, not only do you feel good, but your light makes others feel good. Have you ever walked into a room and didn't know anyone—but as soon as you smiled, someone smiled back? Maybe you visited someone who was sick or sad and as soon as you walked in, they felt better because of you and your beautiful light. Oh, but how about those times when you feel bad? How do you hold up your light then? It's not easy, is it? It's much easier to be the light and let your light shine when you are feeling and looking good. But what about those times when you feel low or when life has knocked you down and nothing is going your way? Or when someone is mean to you or says hurtful things? How do you let your light shine in these situations?

Well, take it from me, you can still be the light and let your light shine in the most difficult times. Even in my current cancer-healing journey, I'm still being the light and letting my light shine. It is during these dark moments you have to remind yourself who you are and the fact that your light never goes away. Think about it. On a cloudy day when you can't see the sun, light is still shining. At night when it is completely dark, the moon still gives off its light. Just like the sun and the moon, your light never disappears. It may be blocked. It may dim. It may even flicker, but it never dissipates. Your light, my beautiful daughter, is always there. It is a part of who you are.

Let me share a few things with you that help me turn up the brightness of my light when things seem dark. First, breathe. Get quiet; take deep, slow breaths, and check in with yourself to see what is really bothering you. Second, figure out what you can do to immediately brighten your light. Dancing or singing usually helps me. Third, try expressing gratitude, praying, laughing, or hugging someone you love. Do something that reminds you how valued you are.

So, my beautiful daughter, I want you to always stand in your light. We need you to shine your light even when it's difficult. Just remember, you can always keep this song in your heart to remind yourself that you are a magnificent, beautiful light. Sing with me please, "This little light of mine, I'm gonna let it shine, let it shine, let it shine, let it shine!"

Keep shining, dear daughters.

Love,

Yolanda Rahman

Precious Jewels,

I challenge you! Know your worth, stay on your seat of power, and never remove your crown! You are the most beautiful female ever created. The Creator specifically fashioned the woman with you in mind. You are truly the example of beauty; an expression of His creative hand, a designer's original. Your enchanted beauty is sacred, with heavenly kisses that glow with an array of angelic tones. It's the diversity of your hair, the curves of your body, the dimensions of your perfectly chiseled face that make your beauty excessively desired. Rightfully so!

Deep within you is an alluring warrior who has yet to be unleashed. As an Afro Woman or should I say, Nubian Queen, you have mysteries hidden within your DNA. You possess within your melanin the mysteries of life, unrevealed secrets to guide you into purpose which was ordained before you were ever created. It is not a mistake that you were born a Black woman. You were placed here with purpose and given a destiny to fulfill. Listen to the data deep within your soul. Connecting to your soul brings a clarity that will manifest into greatness. When you are in harmony with yourself, balance will place you in the position to receive all that has been promised.

Nubian Queen, you are a rare jewel; a precious stone whose formation came from the center of the universe. In you lies the strength and righteous materials that can influence the earth. Your beauty reflects a brilliant ray of light that travels with the spirit of perfection. You are a precious gem, hand-picked and set apart with the highest price; a rare, yet unique design that sparkles upon the earth just as the stars in the sky. Your light is so vivacious it invokes heaven's glory and connects you to the Creator and His universal elements.

So, Queen, let your light shine. You were sent to brighten the world. Never allow your light to be dimmed; your light is your power. Stay in control of your light, embrace your truth, except your flaws, and love yourself. Shine the light of triumph, trailblazing the journey of your soul.

You are the light of the world; the universe's glory. This world is your oyster, and the sky is the limit. Everything you need has been provided. You've been given a position of royalty. You've been adorned with a rainbow of faceted gemstones and polished like diamonds of virtue and honor. This is why the Nubian Woman is highly sought after. Her treasure is envied by many because of the greatness bestowed upon her. It's true! Your beauty, your intelligence, your wisdom, your favor; it's no secret to the universe. From the beginning of time you've been pursued, hunted, and harassed for no known reason except fear. Fear of where you originated. A place rich in culture and pure, with a spirit-filled treasure that is ravishingly glorious.

My beautiful Queen, you are powerful beyond your perception. Open your eyes, see all that has been placed inside of you, and own it. Ground yourself in that power with both of your feet planted firmly on the foundation upon which you were created. Stand firm like a tree planted in the earth, whose roots are strong and secure enough to support its very core.

Beloved, stand in your authentic truth of royalty and power. Never remove your crown! It seals the deal! Every Queen wears her crown decorated with the finest gemstones of the earth, representing victory, triumph, honor and light.

In your honor,

Lisa Collins

Dear Light of the World,

Sometimes we may think we are not pretty enough, important enough, smart enough or influential enough to do what has been placed inside of us to accomplish. For some of us, that could be writing a book about a topic we are passionate about. For others, it could be speaking up more at work, and leading a new effort to bring something new to your workplace. Whatever it is, it has the potential to change lives and change the world. Yes, seriously, sis. Your little idea has the potential to do that but only if you are willing to step forward and let your light shine.

Society has taught Black women and girls that we are limited in what we can do and how we can do it, but we don't have to believe that the depressing statistics and negative stereotypes are true for us. Rather, we can choose to have faith over fear and be that bright spot in an area lacking in hope.

For example, the American Bar Association recently reported that less than 40% of lawyers in the United States are women, and that approximately only 5% of lawyers in the United States are African American. So, it makes sense that at a leadership conference I attended, I met a Black man who was happy to hear that I am a lawyer because he did not know any Black female lawyers. He told me he wanted to take a picture of me to show his 11-year-old daughter that young Black female attorneys exist, and that she could be one as well.

This also goes for you and whatever profession or vocation you are in or choose. No matter your role, we need to show up and be known for our excellence in skill and ability, dedication to our craft, service to the world, and commitment to justice. This is why we cannot let haters, trolls (or even ourselves) take us out of the game. There is so much more good we have left to do in the world, so much more left to accomplish and inspire! So much more light to shine in dark places!

But this letter is not meant to leave you feeling as if you have a burden too heavy for your shoulders. This letter is meant to be an encouragement for you to let your light shine and melanin glisten wherever you are—including in the classroom, boardroom and courtroom. If someone complains that your light is shining too brightly, let them wear shades. Don't tone down your light for anyone. The darkness of fearful thoughts and negativity helps no one. Ramp up the wattage and keep shining. As it says in the ancient text, "You are the light of the world. A town built on a hill cannot be hidden. Neither do people light a lamp and put it under a bowl. Instead, they put it on a stand, and it gives light to everyone in the house. In the same way, let your light shine before others, that they may see your good deeds and glorify your father in heaven" (Matthew 5:14-16 NIV).

You are pretty enough. You are important enough. You are smart enough. You are influential enough. You are the light of the world. Let your light shine.

With love,

Roberta Oluwaseun Roberts

Dear World-Changer,

I am honored to share these words of wisdom as you move towards fulfilling your divine destiny. My beloved, did you know that you are the light of the world? This means your aura, actions, character, and contribution make it known there is something within you that is different. You are uniquely designed to stand out in every room you enter. Understand that God has strategically positioned you to bring light where there is darkness. To bring solutions where there are problems. To bring hope where there is despair. To practice faith where fear abounds. To speak life where there is death. To innovate where industries are antiquated. To break through barriers for the weak. You, my dear, were born to be a legend. You were chosen to be a resource, a problem-solver, and the ultimate world-changer.

Believe it or not, your God-given gifts, skills and talents have all been designed for you to have an impact on an assigned group of people. That's right, people are divinely assigned to you. Your willingness to become the best version of yourself so you can be the light you were meant to be will determine whether you are able to fulfill these assignments. There are friendships you will have to let go, environments you will have to change, and difficult choices you will have to make to ensure you stay on the right path. If you can make the appropriate sacrifices to stay on track, then your light will continue to shine brighter and brighter.

Never let your adversity prevent you from becoming who you were called to be. I was raised in a single-parent household after my father left when I was three. My mom had to be strong and resilient while pursuing a career as a nurse administrator, so she could take care of my two sisters and me. I grew up with all the essentials: food, clothing, shelter, and love, but there was so much more I lacked as a latch-key kid. However, I never let my family background and shortcomings prevent me from being a resource to those around me. I knew I was called to be a leader in my generation. Now, as an author and entrepreneur, I have a platform to change lives and industries for the better. I hope to be an example to you of someone who exudes positivity, humility, and abundant love because of the God in me. I choose to serve others and to be transformed by the renewing of my mind. I choose to be different so I can illuminate the world.

When you let your light shine before others, it does two things: it helps to glorify God, and it gives others permission to step into their greatness and recognize the light within them. Your willingness to shine your light positions you as a person who adds value. Value creation is your ability to step into a situation, identify gaps or opportunities, and provide actionable solutions to fill those gaps. The more frequently and effectively you add value, the more your light shines in the hearts, minds and souls of the people you touch. If you help enough people get to where they need to go, you end up achieving your goal much faster. I leave you with the following affirmations. Speak it out loud: "I am strong. I am powerful. I am destined to impact the world."

I love you!

Your Sister,

Tai Abrams

Section Three

DON'T...

...Doubt Yourself

Dear Sisters,

Don't doubt yourself! You may not be perfect, but you were uniquely created. Remember, none of us are perfect. You may not come from the best home or neighborhood environment. You may not come from a family that supported you (or maybe they didn't know how to support you). Generational curses of addiction, abuse and other negative habits have a chain link that can be broken by you. It may be hard to look past the person in the mirror. You may have struggled with so many things, including your own self-doubt. Don't allow yourself to be the barrier to your own happiness and success.

Don't doubt yourself based on other people's erroneous beliefs about you. Other people may not see your potential or believe in your dream. Other people may speak words or use actions to muddy your thoughts about yourself, which can keep you stuck in self-doubt. Doubt is often deeply rooted in fear. Fear of failure can cause inaction. Fear can cause anxiety and weigh down your footsteps, causing you to stall instead of progressing forward towards change. It is time to celebrate yourself in order to elevate yourself to a level beyond the shadow of your thoughts. It is sometimes hard to pat yourself on the back or praise yourself out loud because of fear of being perceived as arrogant or conceited. The time is now to have confidence in you!

Now is the time to disregard the haters, naysayers, doubters, and those casting judgments. Now is the time to take an inventory of yourself. Self-awareness is a pathway to overcoming self-doubt. Accept that you may have been damaged by something or someone in your past, but you are not damaged beyond repair. Embrace your flaws to strengthen your confidence. Release guilt, anger and hurt to soothe your soul. Forgive yourself and others for your eternal peace of mind. Stop the roller coaster ride in your mind from making dreadful and emotionally draining pit stops by visualizing negative thoughts as dangerous hitchhikers, aiming to rob you of your joy. Talk yourself into loving you no matter what!

You can move past self-doubt. You can use self-talk to motivate and encourage yourself. Words have power, so think positive thoughts and speak positive words on your own behalf. Look in the mirror, smile, and yell if you have to: "You can do it!" Strengthen your support system. Double check your circle of acquaintances and friends. Surround yourself with people who will be honest, but supportive. Be willing to receive constructive criticism that will help you grow. Think about what you can do to improve yourself.

Increase your knowledge by reading material that can promote your own feelings of self-worth and empowerment. Start participating in activities that may be outside of your norm or comfort zone. Accomplishing something that you did not think you could do is powerful, uplifting, and can increase your self-confidence. Don't underestimate small steps because even small steps may be enough to inspire and motivate you to move forward confidently.

Let's not forget the power of prayer. Remember that you are not alone. Believe that you have been granted a unique purpose that has been engraved within you. Renew your faith and start believing in you. Stop doubting and start living to experience a new level of life. Don't doubt yourself!

With love,

Kathrine Henderson

Hello Princess,

I want to tell you about a girl who loved to make mud pies. She loved wetting the dirt and mixing it into mud. In her eyes, those pies were masterpieces. She would play in a mud patch in the front yard of her home. It was not the neatest of hobbies, but she was happy. People young and old would tell her she was wasting her time making mud pies. The girl would laugh and say, "I'm not wasting time if I'm having fun." These same people would tell her to do normal things like everyone else. The girl would always laugh and say, "Being happy is normal."

Soon, their concern turned to insults, "Nobody wants to be around a dirty girl who makes dirty pies. You stink and your clothes are always dirty." The girl, who was wise for her age, just laughed and kept making her mud pies. One day, she looked at her dirty hands, her dirty clothes and her dirty feet. She wondered why making mud pies made other people angry even though it made her happy. She never made a mess beyond her mud patch. She might have gotten mud on her parents' fence, but she always cleaned it up before stepping into the house. She started to think there was something wrong with making mud pies; that something was wrong with her.

One day, the little girl asked her mother, "Why do people have such a big problem with me making mud pies?" Her mother responded, "It's not the mud pies, honey. It's the happiness it gives you." The girl then asked, "Why do they say it's not normal, that I'm not normal? Why do they say nobody wants to be around me? I never mess up the yard, and I always wash my hands and feet before I go inside. Maybe I should stop making mud pies and just do what the other kids are doing." The mother laughed at the little girl and asked, "And end up miserable and unhappy like them?" The girl looked up at her mom and answered "Eww, no!" From that day forward, the girl never doubted what made her happy. She grew up to be a woman who loved making sculptures of pies and other things she loved out of clay.

This girl grew up to discover there were other people like her who loved to play in the mud as children. Some grew up to plant gardens in mud. Some learned how to turn mud into bricks, and bricks into homes. Some loved discovering things in mud. None of them ever strayed from what made them happy.

So, my Princess, there will be something in this life that will make you happy. There will be people who try to make you question what you do and what makes you happy. They will even lie to you and say that nobody will want you because of what you do and who you are. You must remember, my Princess, that many of the people who question your happiness have not yet discovered their happiness. Don't question what makes you happy if it isn't hurting you. Keep pursuing it, whatever it is. You will be amazed at how it will grow and evolve into more things that will make you, and possibly others, happy.

My gift of advice to you is to be like that girl and keep playing in the mud if it makes you happy. Don't let anyone keep you from what brings you joy.

Love,

Maria Josefina Fernandez

To My Beloved Sister,

It is my sincerest hope that this letter finds you in a place where doubt does not exist. I suspect that may not be the case, however. If my suspicion is right, then you are reading this letter at just the right moment. Doubt has this strange way of creeping into our thoughts like a thief in the night. You may ask yourself questions like: "Who am I, do I belong, and can I really do this?" It can grow until you can't tell the difference between doubt and fear. I'm writing this letter to let you know that we all have doubtful moments. It is not that we have doubt, but how we handle it that makes the difference.

I want you to imagine a time when you doubted your ability to do something; then imagine how you felt, what you said, and what you did. The key to changing doubt to confidence is believing in yourself. The questions you should ask yourself are: "What steps do I need to take to accomplish my goal, who can I go to for support, and why am I doubting myself?"

My beloved sister, I would like you to turn your doubt into stepping-stones for success: determination, uniqueness, brilliance, and talent. Determining your outstanding, unique and brilliant talents starts with taking a very critical look at yourself—first through your own eyes, then through the eyes of others. Reflect and think about what is unique or different about you. Your presence in a room should demand attention, letting others know that you have arrived. You understand that all eyes are on you and you embrace that understanding.

When you speak, your voice and words should echo not only the depth of your thoughts, but the brilliance of your mind. It is a way to share the best of you with the world. Speak clearly, my beloved sister, and let your convictions ring with the powerful echoes of our ancestors. You speak for not only yourself, but for those who have come before you and those who will come after you. You speak for the little girl you were and the woman you are becoming. Your voice is like a beacon in the night; lighting the way, blazing a path, and guiding the future of those who need desperately to hear what you have to say. A little girl who is doubting herself is listening, watching, and waiting for you to guide her to a place of hope, inspiration and confidence.

Reach down deep, my beloved sister, and use your talents in a way that supports your hopes, dreams, and aspirations. Always think of your talents as an audition for life, love, and future success. Continue to develop and grow your talents through patience, practice, and passion. They will take you to places you never dreamed of and allow you to accomplish goals and experiences of a lifetime.

I will end my letter to you, my beloved sister, with this thought: Doubt is simply a human way of forcing you to be the very best version of yourself, taking you out of your comfort zone, and helping you realize your greatest dreams, hopes and aspirations. It is your destiny to realize, fulfill and contribute to the powerful legacy of our beloved ancestors, for their most cherished hope was for little Black girls and Black women to truly embrace their power in a way that would leave no doubt as to who they are.

Your beloved sister,

Dr. Angee Valentine

To Light-Skinned Black Girls Who Will Become Light-Skinned Black Women,

Know that you are truly worthy of being a member of the Black race. There are many shades of Black skin, including light and fair complexions like yours. It does not make you less Black, no matter what negative people will tell you. Sadly, some of those negative people will also be Black. Have you already had this happen to you? It can take place in your community, your school, and even in your own family.

Colorism is a form of discrimination or prejudice when light-skinned Blacks are favored over Blacks of darker shades. It is a very unfair and unkind behavior that goes back as far as the era of slavery. However, you are not responsible for that bad behavior, and you should not be judged by it. Never let anyone tell you that you are not Black or not Black enough because of your light skin. Those words are simply untrue. Don't doubt yourself.

If you ever wonder about your worthiness, read about the history of our female heroes. Angela Davis is a civil rights activist, former member of the Black Panthers, and a fierce light-skinned Black woman. During the 1970s, she rocked a huge afro and fought for racial and gender equality. Rosa Parks, who you may have already learned about in school, was a petite, but strong light-skinned Black woman. By refusing to give up her seat on a public bus to a white man, she set the Montgomery Bus Boycott in motion, which changed segregation laws.

Davis and Parks did not allow anyone to question their Blackness. They stood up to people of all races. Although your path in life may differ from these women, you can still be just as proud of your racial background. Davis said, "I am no longer accepting the things I cannot change. I am changing the things I cannot accept." Young ladies, what will you accept or not accept as you grow up? Parks did not have any children, but she is quoted as saying, "Racism is still with us. But it is up to us to prepare our children for what they have to meet and hopefully, we shall overcome."

Whether you have to deal with racism from non-Blacks or Blacks, neither one is okay. Be ready to show strength. Use your self-esteem as your self-defense against them.

You probably have heard the phrase "Black girl magic" which began gaining popularity in 2013. It is often used to describe the beauty, power and uniqueness of Black females regardless of their size, shape, or shade. Celebrities, motivational speakers, professional athletes and more are using the phrase to describe the talents and accomplishments of Black women and girls.

What does Black girl magic mean to you? Hopefully, it means positivity and inspiration for all shades of Black skin. When you become an adult, you can write a letter like this to young Black girls and tell them all about it.

Sincerely,

Kimberly H. Smith

My Dearest Beloved,

I write this letter with a sincere wish for you to remove all doubt and lack of trust in yourself; instead, garner peace, joy, security, and patience in your life. In this complex world in which we live, there is always an aspect of doubt peeking around the corner. Doubt is used as a tactic to redirect you, throw you off course, or plant insecurity in your mind. Do not let it take root in your body, mind, and soul. It is important to keep your eyes on the prize and keep focused on the main thing. We all have doubts, such as: "Do I deserve this new, healthy relationship? Will I be successful in the new job? Will I be able to manage motherhood and marriage?"

The answer depends on you. You have the choice to be hindered by doubt or use past struggles and disappointments as lessons for growth. You have the choice to turn former misery into victories in your life by tackling them head on and understanding the role you played in the situation. You will need to reframe your thinking, focus your energy outward, and leave no room for the cultivation of uncertainty in your heart, spirit, and soul. Imagine your greatness, dream your dreams, and constantly remind yourself how smart, beautiful and creative you are. Reflect on the fact that a setback in life is only a pause to hear God whispering words of encouragement and cheering you on to the victory line of success. That is why you will want to surround yourself with positive, motivated, enthusiastic people who bring rays of light into your circle. Whenever you experience doubts, you will have to be patient. Is patience easy? No.

Patience requires silence; applying listening skills, being careful to listen to the right voice, praying for clarity, and understanding that all things happen for a reason and at different seasons in your life. Sometimes "no" is the answer to a desired want because it may not be the best thing for you. It may not be the time or season for something to happen. That "no" could protect you from danger down the road.

Secure wise counsel from people who have your best interest in mind. When you are being patient and waiting, pray for direction and guidance, and the best course of action you should take. I am convinced that if you exercise patience—peppered with grace and understanding—you will make the right decisions and remove self-doubt.

Whether you doubt the new man who came into your life, the high-power job you worked so hard for, or your ability to parent the child you've been blessed with; embrace it, accept it, and give praise. Celebrate the small steps, keep the victories coming, and reflect on the fact that self-doubt freezes you in time, space and motion. It prevents you from living your best life. Do not get trapped into comparing yourself to someone else. You are unique and wonderfully made, with a glorious story to tell. I will be watching and waiting to hear about your great experience in life. Beloved, now go forth and do great things!

Love,

Dr. Jacqueline Bingham Flemmings

...Be Afraid to Fail

To My Beautiful Queens,

Has the fear of failure stopped you from living out your potential and learning what life truly has to offer you? In life, we create goals that we set out to achieve, asserting our maximum potential and effort with no room for failure. We set high standards and seek to raise the bar every step of the way. But what I've learned is that with success comes failure in some form or fashion. Failure is a thing we steer clear of because we don't want to appear weak in the eyes of others, and we believe that success is the only acceptable outcome. Failure is a potential outcome and should be considered in every plan, goal, and vision. Being open to the possibility of failure and embracing the lessons learned allows us as women to live fearlessly and walk boldly into our destiny. Being fearless is embracing failure as a possible outcome, using the experience to propel you in your next endeavor, and allowing it to highlight your strengths and weaknesses.

Failure activates our strength and determination, which allows us to persevere in the face of adversity. Don't be afraid of failure; embrace it and challenge yourself to learn from it. Many successful women like Oprah Winfrey (Chairwoman of OWN) and Melissa Butler (Founder and CEO of the Lip Bar) have experienced failure before success, but they used it to propel them forward rather than allowing it to hold them back. Life will throw you many obstacles and trials in the form of failure but what you do with it will determine your success in life.

As women, we are often stricken with the superwoman complex, which I describe as believing we have to do everything ourselves in order for our vision to come to fruition. We shoulder all the responsibilities, tasks and burdens because we fear that if we don't do it, it won't be done correctly, or even worse, the plan will fail. I suffered from the superwoman complex and, at times, failed even harder because I didn't ask for help. I later learned there were many women willing to share their wisdom and experience to help me achieve success. That made my journey much more meaningful. Instead of taking on that superwoman complex, look to your sisters and don't be too prideful or fearful to seek guidance or a helping hand. Let's develop a sisterhood where we strengthen and lift each other up in times of failure.

I challenge you to embrace failure, not run from it or allow it to stop you from pursuing your dreams, goals, or destiny. Your destiny is much bigger than any failure you may face. Treat each failure as a stepping-stone to your greatness and pursue your purpose in life with vigor and determination.

If we are afraid to pursue our dreams because of fear of failure, we may never see the greatness that lies within. There is value in failure, and I believe you are strong enough to push through fear. If you need encouragement or inspiration, know that I am standing with you!

With love,

Jamillah Smith

Dear Young Queen,

I will be the first to tell you that failure feels awful. I will be the first to admit that the first time I failed at something, I felt inadequate. I will be the first to share that I have wept bitterly in the face of failure, and I will be the first to tell you about my scars.

I will also be the first to tell you I got up, I healed, I became resilient. I survived, and I thrived. Failure seems to be the antithesis of success; but I believe that failure works in tandem with success. So, my Queen, I say to you, don't be afraid to fail.

My first encounter with failure as an emotional tie occurred when I was 11 years old and failed a science class. That encounter was the genesis of my process of learning how to get up and live, despite not attaining success. I am a living testament that success follows failure.

Failure is a numbers game. Many of the world's greatest athletes have had some of the largest number of failures. How can this be? It is because they have a high number of attempts. An attempt can end in a success or a failure. The key is that an attempt must be made. When failure comes, you have choices. You can give up, retreat, or try again.

Queen, I will state the obvious. Giving up is the least desirable choice you can make after you fail. There is so much that you lose when you give up. Look around you. What do you see? You see a demonstration of many types of technology and creativity; from the clothes you're wearing to the device you may be using to read this text. Wow, the wonders of technology! But wait! Much of what you are seeing and experiencing is because people did not give up after their first failure. They did not stop, throw up their hands and say, "I am done! It didn't work!" Instead, they tried again and again until they got it right, and now you are reaping the benefits of someone else's failure and their refusal to give up. Take that in. The luxuries you are enjoying now are because another individual decided not to give up, so don't be afraid to fail.

Failing may make you feel as if you want to retreat or return to your previous state of being. To return is to stunt your growth, and as a result, someone will not be a recipient of the gifts that have been bestowed upon you. Those gifts will only be released if you keep trying. In other words, people need you to push beyond your failure, so your talent and abilities can bless them. Do not minimize the impact and difference you can make in another person's life. Don't be afraid to fail.

Queen, expect the success but be ready for the failure. The doors will close; your applications will be rejected, and many will flat out tell you "no." But remember, the more you hear "no," the closer you get to the "yes." Do not be afraid to fail. You have value. You have worth. You are miraculous. Not all will see these qualities in you, but it does not change who you are. The world is waiting. The world needs you. Don't be afraid to fail.

Love,

Vuyanzi Rodman

To Girls Struggling to Meet Their Goals,

"Courage allows the successful woman to fail and learn powerful lessons from the failure, so that in the end, she didn't fail at all." —Maya Angelou

My mum used to tell me that my best was good enough. My interpretation of that was this: my best is good enough to succeed, so if I'm not succeeding, I must not be trying hard enough. Hearing that was a huge burden. It gave birth to self-loathing and frustration that I was not better than who and what I was. I was afraid of producing something subpar, so I would rarely complete a project. I would see the shiny, finished projects of others, look at my dull, half-finished works, then shove them in a place where no one could see.

Life will do that to you. In the media, we see gorgeous models, actors, and the most talented singers the world has to offer. We see famous paintings that revolutionized their industry. We see their amazing finished projects—look at our own work in progress—and feel inferior. We're afraid that at completion, ours will never be able to stand next to the greats. But success grows out of the lessons that come with failure.

As an artist, I follow artists that I and many others look up to. While looking at their professional art is inspiring, it's also intimidating. How could I possibly create art that perfectly? Someone else who also felt this inadequacy confronted one artist: "How are your doodles so perfect every time you draw?" I waited eagerly for the answer: "It's more like I make a ton of doodles, and then only show the good ones." That answer really impacted me. Her success grew out of multiple failures, but we only saw the success. When you look down at your own incomplete project, confident that you won't be able to succeed, remember that every person you look up to has stared down at their incomplete project just as you are now. Failure isn't an end—it's a step.

As a Black woman in this country, you are going to experience obstacles incomprehensible to those who don't have them. Sometimes, you're going to feel that your failure is more devastating than those of a different skin tone, sex or gender—but there are no two people with the same experiences, and your experiences are what make you uniquely you. It's impossible to fairly compare yourself to others because your circumstances are not the same. "We've both been dancing for six years, but he's so much better than me!" "My grades will never be as good as hers!" Well, he had lessons, and you taught yourself. You have two jobs, while she's able to study all day. There will always be a difference between you and someone else, so it isn't fair—and it certainly isn't fruitful—to compare. What you can compare is your current self to your past self. Am I getting better? What can I do to move forward? I've failed again; how will this experience lead me toward success? Don't berate but be gentle with yourself. The famed poet, Nikki Giovanni, said "Mistakes are a fact of life. It is the response to the error that counts."

It took a very long time for me to realize what my mum meant when she told me that my best was good enough. It was good enough not because if I try my best, I will always succeed—but because trying my best is success. Your best is good enough. Your best is success. Failure is not an end, because success grows out of the lessons that come with failure.

Wishing you success,

R.A. Leigh Hawkins

Dear Young Sister,

Failure is the process you go through when you attempt to accomplish a goal. Often, we focus on the negative rather than the positive. I guess you are wondering, "What is positive about failure?" The answer is the experience and the lessons learned while working towards a certain goal. The phrase "Today is the first day of the rest of your life" is important, because it provides confirmation that it is acceptable to start over again. Most people get so focused on winning or achieving a goal, they don't realize there are hidden jewels in the experiences and lessons learned with failure. When you think of the word *fail*, what comes to mind? When I think of the word fail, I think of this: Focus and Accept the Important Lesson.

Focusing is a key aspect to accomplishing any goal. This is the time in your life when you need a one-track mind to keep an eye on the prize. My young sister, there are so many distractions with modern technology that provide what I call "smoke and mirrors." The term "smoke and mirrors" refers to an illusion, or something that appears to be one way, but it is not. For example, have you ever had a bad day, logged on to social media, and it seems as if everyone is living their best life? If you answered yes, did you ever think the person's page you viewed could be stretching the truth to make themselves look better in society's eyes? It is up to you to be strong, confident, and focused on your goal rather than comparing yourself to your best friend or a celebrity. This is when the phrase "stay in your own lane" applies.

Accept the mistake made and use it to your advantage. You can think of it as a process of elimination. If you had four options and the one you selected was wrong, then the answer lies within the remaining three. This process helps you get closer to reaching your goals. In life, the worst thing you can do is give up on your goals. In fact, this is when you should work even harder and ignore those who say you should give up. You will notice that sometimes the people closest to you might be cheering for the opposite team.

Important is a word that is used frequently, but I want you to use it as an adjective to describe yourself. When you look in the mirror, I want you to see a beautiful and important young woman who is not afraid to fail. My young sister, you are of value, and the lessons you are learning—whether positive or negative—are valuable too!

Lessons are a learning tool. They can be a powerful tool if you have the right mind-set. My young sister, no one ever said that life will be easy, but it is what you make out of it. When you encounter an unfavorable outcome, understand that the lesson learned can be used as an example of what not to do. Please be mindful that it is normal to fail; in fact, you may even fall, but the key is to get up, dust yourself off, and try again!

Allow the word *fail* to be used to motivate and encourage you when you feel like giving up. You are not alone. I am here, cheering you on! Remember to focus and accept the important lesson!

Love, your big sister,

Dr. Ashley Valentine

Sis,

She lost herself. She was being everyone else's savior, while her soul was yearning for saving. People used her temple as a safe haven. And once restored, they'd be no more. She asked God, "Why me? Am I fulfilling what you created me to be?" Sis, I am she.

If you are anything like me, you probably question why you are here. Why now, why this, why today? Maybe you wish that God would come sit next to you and tell you the plan for your life. Maybe you question why if "no weapon formed against you, shall prosper," you experience so much pain (Isaiah 54:17 NKJV). Why do those you trust turn their back on you? Why does it feel as if you'll never become what you were called to be? Maybe you question if there is even a purpose for your life.

When I asked God these questions, He gave me a reply. He told me it was all necessary. Here's the reason. Sis, you have to be prepared for what you've been called to do. See, purpose doesn't come without challenges, and you have to be able to withstand the tests. But with every test, you are building a testimony that will help another sister overcome. God is protecting you from far more than you'll ever know; accidents, people, broken promises, even places you should not go. I've learned a lesson I hope will help you. Even though you may feel alone and like nothing is going well, God is within you, and because of that, you cannot fail.

Yes, you will experience scars and bruises; but they do not determine your worth. There will be times when you want to scream, and nothing will come out. God is there with you in the deafening silence. Things that you thought were good for you will fall away. People who you thought were good to you, will change their ways. Remember, you've been set apart, not set aside—but sometimes they look and feel the same. But there will be a shift. Your elevation will come, and everything you lost will be restored.

I want you to know that good things are in the works for you, so don't be afraid to fail. When you let go of how you think life should be, you make room for what needs to happen. Every time you feel rejected by someone or something that looks good, trust that you are being redirected to something greater! Focus on the brightest of days and hold on to hope in the darkest of days.

You are not alone. God is with you, and so am I.

Love,

Kurshay Whitaker

...Be Afraid to Start Over

To My Apprehensive, Audacious Sisters,

I hear you are starting over. Congratulations! Don't be afraid or dismayed. Whatever the circumstances were that brought you to this point in your life are in the past. It's history. Yeah! You get a new beginning (somewhat a privilege, I'd say). You get to make different choices and decisions for your life than in the past. There may be an addition of people, places and things, or a subtraction of the same required.

Various emotions could arise. Rise above them and press on. Put on your big girl panties and forge forward. Begin again. It's possible. In fact, it's critical. Consider what other paths you can take.

You may encounter resistance at every angle. Allow it to catapult you ahead. You may or may not have the support of the people in your circle (family or friends). Don't let this discourage you. Be your own cheerleader. Remember, it's your life, your journey and your future.

You may question yourself. "Can I do this? How do I start? What do I do first? What can or cannot happen?" The unknown can be daunting, yet possible to navigate with determination and true grit. Pull from the strength inside of you. Employ your talents. Rely on those good character traits you have. Know yourself. You'd be surprised what a "can-do, won't quit" attitude can accomplish.

Get moving. Put one foot in front of the other and walk it out. Remember, every time a foot goes down, it touches foundation.

You may be getting older, but age is not a factor. If anything, it's a plus. Over the years, you've gained wisdom, knowledge, and strength. You can extract from all you have seen, heard, and experienced for your start over.

Make the best of your journey. Approach it with great expectations and the willingness to make any necessary adjustments along the way to ensure your transition is smooth as possible. Be patient. It will be a process; solicit help when needed. Whatever your objective, there are resources available to aid in achieving your expected end.

May you approach your start over with fearlessness.

Be of good courage.

Your sister who also started over,

Carolyn Griffin

Dear Queen!

I am you, and you are me. I see you. I know you. I understand you. Don't be afraid to start over. I've been where you are. The beginning point of a start over is beautiful, wonderful, and exciting. You've been here before, and here you are again. It's not as scary as you think.

Every moment of your life creates sentences that end and start anew, and paragraphs that eventually create the chapters of your life story. Think about it. Without a new start, your story would be incomplete. Every time you open your eyes, it is the beginning of seeing something new. When you awaken from sleep, your body starts over. Each day is a new start. It's your chance at a new opportunity. What happened yesterday is behind you; the mess-ups, the mistakes and goals that weren't achieved. There are lessons to learn, and gratitude to express for what was and what you will carry with you into the next start over.

You've arrived now! You're here at a new beginning. It could be starting a class, a new school, a new business, a new relationship, a new career, or a new life. Every new start brings you to a higher level with higher-level challenges that are part of the journey leading to your destiny. Those things you lost and sacrificed were all part of the process to get you closer to where you're supposed to be, what you're supposed to have, and to give you a better appreciation for everything you've overcome and achieved.

Every new start will bring you closer to knowing who you are; owning the power of who you are and the purpose for which you were called. There is a purpose for everything that happens in your life. This is your life. You have the power to take action.

You get to decide what happens next. You got knocked down. You decide to get up. You failed. You decide on the next step, the next strategy. You were told no. You decide not to take no for an answer. You were told you're not good enough. You decide you are good enough. You were told what you can't do. You decide what you can do. You were told you can't have a seat at the table. You decide to create your own table. Take the necessary actions to make it happen. You have sistas who are with you and here to help you.

You have the power to reinvent yourself! You have a fresh beginning to determine the next chapter of your life. You get to be creative. Who do you want to be? What life do you want? You can create it! You get to renew, reenergize, and reclaim what's yours. You get to express yourself in new ways. You get a do-over every day you are among the living. You are a unique gift. Your life is a gift to the world. The Bible says, "For God has not given us a spirit of fear and timidity, but of power, love, and self-discipline" (2 Timothy 1:7 NLT). So, go forward without fear!

This is your time to do what you are called to do, to become who you were called to be, and to live the life of your dreams! Start now!

Love,

Shante R. Roddy

Hey Girlfriend!

Allow me to be the first to congratulate you. If you are reading this letter, it means you have lived a little, made some choices, and can probably admit (if you're being honest with your girlfriend) that you've screwed up a few things. So, why the congratulations, you ask? Because that's what friends do! Plus, you didn't give up and are still standing! You've taken the first step necessary to begin again! You get a "do-over" for everything you feel you've failed. I know what you're thinking, "But I really messed up this time." I say, "So what!" Me too; I'm living proof that no matter how bad you think it is, starting over and being successful can be your reality. Don't look at it like you're starting from scratch; but picking up where you left off with more experience. Don't be afraid to start over.

Feeling afraid is normal. But if it's the driving factor that keeps you stuck and prevents you from moving forward, then it is the real challenge. Just remember, you're reading this because you want to make moves, but it's easier to make excuses because it's scary to take the first step. So, be encouraged. We're in this together. Check your hand. I know it's probably sweaty, and that's ok. If it is, just wipe it dry. Reach out your hand and gently take mine. We will do it together, girlfriend.

Okay. So, let's go a little deeper. There are many things we fear about starting over; however, let's talk about the fear of the unknown. Let's face it, it's tough to start anything when you can't foresee the outcome. Your routine is safe and comfortable, but anything worth having in life requires shaking that up a bit. You will never know if you don't try.

When you start a new journey in your life, it's your chance to do things differently. You don't need a new day. Just a new mindset. How? Think about the worst-case scenario. I know. It may not sound like the best advice, but if you're prepared for the worst, then what can really surprise you? Not much. It's not about being negative or predicting failure. It's more about convincing yourself that even if everything crashes, your world will still keep turning, and there is a way out. That kind of positive mindset is crucial when starting over and will lead you in the right direction.

There are many times in our lives when we start over—especially as a woman—that demand grit, passion and perseverance. Whether it comes in the form of illness, parenting, divorce, job change, business failure, loss of a loved one, or going to prison, there is a time when you realize the only way through it is going through it.

That time for me was a combination of all the above. Girlfriend; talk about things moving so fast it makes your head swim! I was drowning. I am an expert at starting over. After being released from prison, I had to learn how to make responsible decisions when I had never made one of those in my life. I chose to believe in myself yet again. I did it afraid at first, and so can you! Don't be afraid to start over. Living your best life is at stake.

When starting over, don't give up. You own the fear; it doesn't own you. If at first you don't succeed, redefine success. I'm still holding your hand, girlfriend.

Love,

Allison T. Garrett

Dear Young, Black Woman,

Don't be afraid to start over. There will come a time when you feel as if you must make a decision to start over. You will have varying degrees of emotions that range from excitement, fear, doubt, anxiety, peace and finally, certainty. You may even have some people in your life who may discourage you from starting over. It is your decision and yours alone to make. You have to ask yourself, "What is best for me?" It may be that you realized the person you are with is not a good fit for you emotionally. It's time to start over. It may be accepting a promotion that requires you to live in a new city or state. It's time to start over. It may be changing careers altogether because you realize you can do more for yourself and your family. It's time to start over.

Don't be afraid to start over.

Many times, we start over without even realizing it. Such as when you go off to college. Leaving behind family and friends you are familiar with can be intimidating and frightening. However, it has been stated over and over again, that your college friends become your lifelong friends. These will be the same people you can turn to in moments of grief and celebration. Embrace the change and welcome new people into your life.

Don't be afraid to start over.

There will be times in your life when you question your purpose in life. You may wonder if what you are doing is worthwhile for your future. You may need to make drastic changes: relocate, change professions or start a new business. During these times, which some refer to as a "mid-life crisis," try not to think of it as a crisis—but as a turning point in your life. Shift your thinking from negativity to the endless possibilities. It's not a crisis, but a breakthrough. Breaking through to find your purpose.

Starting over can be frightening and downright scary. However, if you have the right mindset, starting over can be an adventure that is full of wonder and accomplishments. Think about it this way: starting over can be likened to riding a rollercoaster. When you are in line at the amusement park waiting your turn, you're excited, scared, nervous, and sometimes full of bravado. As you get closer to the ride, those feelings increase. Will you go through with it and get on the ride? Or will you turn around and wait for your friends on the ground? Life can be like a rollercoaster; never knowing what bend, dip, or drop is waiting for you, but it is also exhilarating and breathtaking.

I've chosen to live my life to the fullest. Starting over is part of living. I have many friends who've stated they wish they were more like me—willing to take risks and start over. I don't want to look back on my life and say, "I wish I would have done that," or "I should have done that." I don't want you to have those regrets either. Don't be afraid to start over. Get on the rollercoaster and go for the ride. You could be missing the greatest adventure of your life.

With love,

Dr. Marla Wormley

Dear Sister Friend,

You are on my mind heavy today. I have so much to share with you but at this moment, we will talk about the beauty of starting over without fear. Starting over can be as simple as ripping up an essay and starting on a fresh sheet of paper or it can be as complicated as uprooting your life and walking away from toxic family and friends. Or, it could land somewhere in the middle, like having to build a new skill set to get a new job.

In each of these scenarios, there is an emotional component that leads to the desire or need to start over, and there is likely an emotion triggered by the start over. These emotions need to be processed. Emotions play a big part in preparing your next move. How you process your emotions dictate the direction your decisions will take, but sometimes it's hard to step back from the emotion to determine the best way to maneuver through your start over. The number one emotion that comes with starting over is fear. Fear takes over when we don't know what's going to happen, and it creeps in when our confidence is low. Having to start over can leave you feeling vulnerable and less confident than you were before. So, what do you do?

Create a plan and lay it out step by step. Don't just let things happen; let me tell you why. When you write it out step by step, you force yourself to think things through more deeply, which may help you view things differently. Remember, whatever change you are resisting is a blessing in disguise. Change is usually what you need to take your life to the next level of your journey. You are starting over for a reason. Lift and leverage what you learned from the pain and use it to fuel your confidence and drown out the fear.

OK, so now you have a detailed plan outlining the steps you need to take—however, you still need to work through your emotions. You still need to face your fears. Your fears may never appear in physical form, but they are still there. Journaling is a great way to identify, face, and overcome your fears. I'm going to share my journaling framework with you to help you get started. I use it every day to check in with my thoughts and feelings. Take a piece of paper and write the following prompts:

Moment: How am I honoring the moment, and finding the joy in my day?

Motion: How am I moving my body so that it gets what it needs today?

Message: What am I saying to myself about myself?

Mood: How am I feeling today?

If your responses to the prompts are not positive, take a moment to honor those feelings, then rewrite the narrative. What can you do in this moment to change your perspective and your feelings? Here's a tip. Your thoughts influence your feelings. If you change a thought to something positive, you'll find that your feelings will lean in the same direction. I wanted you to walk away with a tool you can use that could help jumpstart your next chapter. Feeling fear is normal, but don't let it consume you to the point where you become dysfunctional and indecisive. Don't be afraid to start over. Enjoy the process of starting over. I promise you, the only story you'll want to read a year from now is the one you wrote a year ago.

Be well on purpose,

Traci R. Green

To My Dear Sister with the Melanin Hue,

Your moment of starting over is an adventure awaiting you! Oh, I didn't always feel like that; but from experience, I noticed that when I created a positive perception of the various circumstances I faced, I grew. Each circumstance challenged and encouraged me to learn about and use time management, organizational skills, my available resources, and good communication techniques. Now, I am not saying that starting over is easy or comfortable, and in many cases the reason behind the need to make a change totally catches us off guard. However, "Maybe it's not always about trying to fix something that is broken. Maybe it's about starting over and creating something better." —Unknown

You may initially cry enough tears to fill a river. My tears soothed me temporarily, but they didn't help me in the mechanics of moving forward. You may feel angry a time or three and find yourself asking out loud, "Why me?" That's when I realized I had an opportunity to become the captain of this ship and navigate the flow of each scenario. Your Higher Power will help you avoid extensive anguish, fear, confusion and stress. You are not alone; do not trick yourself into thinking you are. Pick up the phone and call a friend or seek professional help. You will never know what help or resources are available to you if you keep things to yourself. Please don't worry. Nine times out of ten, the awful scenario the enemy designs in your mind won't happen. You must tell negative thoughts to get lost, brush the worry off your shoulders, and stomp on them. Yes, literally! Ha ha! It feels so good!

By all means, get out of the house—even if you'd rather sit in the dark with the covers pulled over your head. Visit a church or synagogue; you do not have to be religious to go in and inhale its beauty and peace. Visit a park, art museum, library, or shopping malls (even people-watching can be refreshing and hilarious). Just get out of the house. These things can help you focus or refocus, whichever you need to do at the time.

I encourage you to take a few deep, slow, cleansing breaths before you create that positive perception I mentioned earlier. Grab a piece of paper and a pencil (you may like to use your computer or tablet and that's fine, but in my opinion, when you take time to write something down, it becomes more mentally concrete). Pencils are also great because you can easily erase, and there is no chance of anything accidentally being deleted! Focus on the type of start over that is necessary. Do you need to relocate, change schools, find a new job, downsize, get married or divorced, become a caregiver, etc.? Begin by creating a list of pros and cons; and as you make calls and appointments, I recommend you pray in your own way to your Higher Power for each contact to be with the right person with the right temperament. Write their name, the date, and time you spoke, and the outcome of the conversation.

> "You may encounter many defeats, but you must not be defeated. In fact, it may be necessary to encounter the defeats, so you can know who you are, what you can rise from, how you can still come out of it."
>
> —Maya Angelou

You've got this! You are resilient!

From someone who cares,

Dee Outler

...Give Up

Hello My Queen,

I am enthusiastically writing this letter to you as a message of hope and encouragement. There is a level of excitement and anticipation for you, and I hope that this letter catapults you forward. I am honored to have the opportunity to plant a seed, or water what's already been planted in you. I'm not sure what season you're currently in and you may be in a season where it feels like there is uncertainty. Maybe you're in a season where you feel you have tried to do everything by the book but—in all your labor—things still aren't working together as planned. You may be praying for things to change, or searching for an answer, yet experiencing radio silence. You may be hoping for a new beginning but feel stuck in the same-old-same-old. You've been tempted to throw your hands up and say, "Forget it, I'm done!" You don't see change coming. You're frustrated! You're anxious! You are done!

I want to encourage you today: Don't give up! Look in the mirror and tell yourself "Don't give up, you have too much to offer!" You have too much to give, and you are too special! You are too beautiful! You are too talented! You are too skilled! You are too amazing to give up, and you are fearfully and wonderfully made. All of this qualifies you to win! In the end, you need to know you were destined to win, so you cannot give up!

Michelle Obama stated, "Every girl, no matter where she lives, deserves the opportunity to develop the promise inside of her." While you may feel that your new beginning or your answer is delayed, rest assured you are in the development process. You are being pruned and groomed for greater! You are being prepared for the next! So, stick with it! Stay in the race! Don't throw in the towel! Don't abandon the dream! Don't let go! Don't retreat! Don't abort the idea! Better yet, just don't give up!

I love you, and I pray this letter reaches you at the right time, in the midst of your situation when a timely word is needed!

Love, your sister,

Dr. Malaika Turner

To My Purpose-filled Sister!

"Every great dream begins with a dreamer. Always remember, you have within you the strength, the patience, and the passion to reach for the stars to change the world." —Harriet Tubman

Blessed are you who are called to complete a purpose in this world only you can fulfill. Your purpose predates your existence. You were created to be the solution to a problem in the world only you can solve. If you reached the point of giving up, it means you already identified what you are passionate about and have taken steps toward completing your goal. Don't give up now!

Remember your "why!" Your why is that initial flicker of flame that was lit inside of you, and that your passion won't let die. Your why produces the guilt and shame you feel when you submit to challenges that rise and push your purpose to the side. Your why is the solution to an injustice you see in the world that you cannot overlook. Your why is bigger than you, and sometimes causes you to doubt your ability to make a difference. Your why is the root of your passion, and your passion propels you forward into purpose. Meditate on your why; it is what will sustain you as you push through your weariness!

We all have experienced the desire to give up and if you ever held on and endured the painful process, you know that just on the other side of your worst days are your best days! Just as flowers do not bloom without rain, notable success does not occur without sweat, tears, and pain. Trial and tribulations will come to deter you but count it all joy! When you run into adversity, let that be encouragement to you. If what you were producing did not have value, you would not have opposition. It is my belief that God has a plan for each of us, and when we align ourselves with our purpose, the enemy does all he can to kill, steal, and destroy the vision we were given.

Conquer your fear! Experience has shown me that fear is a tool of discouragement, used to keep you from being successful in what you were purposed to do in life. I encourage you to shift your mindset when you encounter fear. Although your natural reaction to fear is to run away, don't. When fulfilling a goal, fear should cause you to do the opposite. Let fear be your fuel and propel you forward. There is a version of you that can only be produced when you face your fears. Something new must be developed in you for you to conquer what you once viewed as a limitation.

Have faith! It takes faith for you to walk head-first into a challenging situation, or unfamiliar territory. If you were called to your purpose, your adamant "yes" will get you through. The world is awaiting your yes. Yes, to your purpose, and all the challenges that will appear as you walk unapologetically in pursuit of your goal. As you push past doubt, worry and fear, you will see that success is right on the other side! Don't give up!

Your sister in love,

NaTasha Tierra

Dear Beautiful Black Sister,

Do you feel too afraid to follow your dreams? Are you afraid of defeat or has self-doubt made your dreams feel hopeless? Has pain, brokenness, and unfortunate life circumstances crushed your spirit? I'm here to tell you that pain and fear come in your life to steal and destroy dreams. But "Be strong and do not give up, for your work will be rewarded" (2 Chronicles 15:7 NIV). God has equipped you with everything you need to succeed, despite your circumstances!

There are things in life you'll experience that will leave feelings of great pain, trauma, and grief that you feel are destroying your dreams. These are the times in your life when you want to give up and let all your dreams die. I know that pushing past these feelings seems too hard, and probably downright impossible. You may feel abandoned, alone, and like all hope of a great future is lost. Trust me, I've been there. I lost my sister and father during my first year of law school and had to take a leave of absence to get through immense grief. You feel like giving up is the only option you have, because life pushed you so far down. What do you do when you feel emotionally bankrupt and ready to give up?

The answer is to use the courage God gave you and push forward, anyway. Courage is the ability to do something even though you are afraid; being strong, despite your pain or grief. Pain and grief will tell you that whatever happened in your life is too much to allow you to succeed, that you are incapable of moving forward and destined for failure. The fear of failure will take over your mind and you'll believe the lies that your pain tells you about yourself and your future. It is difficult to have the courage to stand up for yourself and fight for your dreams against all the pain you feel. It takes courage to say no to self-doubt. It takes courage to say no to the fear of failure. But the only real failure in life is to stop trying, to stop living, and to stop moving forward. If you are blessed to wake up tomorrow, you have another opportunity to take a step towards your dreams. You can be very afraid, and still stand up to fear!

You may want to fold under all the pressure and pain. You can call on your higher power to give you the strength you don't have. God has almighty power and has placed that same power in you to overcome the pain inside of you. As you continue to move forward, working towards your goals and dreams, your fear will subside, and your strength will take over. Fear has no choice but to step aside when you see yourself accomplishing small goals on the way to your ultimate success. You will feel a little less afraid each step of the way until you have kicked fear's butt!

Many people you looked up to have probably faced a time when they felt like giving up. If they would have caved into those feelings, they would not be where they are today. That is because feelings are temporary; they don't last forever. That's why you can't give them power. I chose not to give up by leaning on my faith in God to push past grief; and went back and finished law school! Choose not to give up. Your greatness is right around the corner.

Love,

Janell S. Foster

Dear Sister,

It's so worth it, my dear, to keep plugging away and seeing what's on the other side of the obstacle, challenge, or barrier making you want to throw in the towel and give up. I beg of you, don't do it. Life is filled with daily surprises (both good and bad) making life all the more interesting. Take the opportunity to show the world you are built for whatever comes your way.

I've always made the choice to defy the odds or written requirements and figure out how to work around the rules in a positive way. When you read that job description and it asks for a qualification you may not fully meet, apply anyway. When you are invited to a special meeting or group and start to feel like you shouldn't be in that room, know that you belong there, and don't give up on yourself or question why you're there. Don't doubt or give up on yourself; you deserve to be wherever the divine plan for your life takes you.

To ensure that you don't give up, from time to time you will have to make choices to eliminate people and things in your life that counter what you should be doing to move forward. Individuals who have no desire to keep fighting and finding out what's on the other side of "no," or who feel they simply cannot overcome an obstacle, will sometimes advise you to quit, or try dragging you down. Those individuals should be removed from your life or placed in a different category of relationship.

There are certain negative environments you may find yourself in; make it a point to remove yourself from those spaces immediately. Place yourself in or create environments that feed your soul, encourage positive thoughts, and support you as you move forward to achieve your goals.

There are so many quotes, songs, and images that exemplify the willing spirit that does not give up on itself. Surround yourself with written or visual examples of what it is to keep moving and not give up.

After a cancer diagnosis I received in 2018, I made a decision to defy the diagnosis. Moving forward in life, I'm committed to defying the rejection, the norms, and the negativity that comes as I continue to fight this disease with everything I have, while accomplishing the goals I've set for myself. One Bible verse I love comes from Galatians 6:9 (NKJV): "And let us not be weary in well doing: for in due season we shall reap, if we faint not."

I advise you to celebrate yourself daily, don't give up, and consider the many places a changed, made up mind will take you.

Wishing you continued peace and an abundance of blessings throughout life's journey.

With love,

Tynetta T. Brown

To My Beautiful Black Butterflies,

I am writing this love letter to encourage you to never give up. Always dream, and then add the corresponding determination and drive to ensure your desires are manifested. My hope is that, as you read through this love letter and all the other pages penned by beautiful Black women, you realize the potential your life holds and the impact you can and will make in the earth realm as you take responsibility for your existence, and become purposeful with your life choices.

My passion as a little girl was to become a teacher. I always saw myself as someone who enjoyed learning, and that passion evolved into advocating for educational equality. Eventually I became an educational entrepreneur, launching my business in August 2019.

The beauty within my story and success that I hope inspires you, is knowing that it started with very humble beginnings as the third child born to a very young single mother, and who was raised in a housing project. I had dreams and goals as an enthusiastic little girl that eventually took longer to achieve than I anticipated because of challenges and choices made along my journey. However, my desire for education—though delayed—was not denied. Hard work pays great dividends!

My letter of love is to remind you of the strength you possess, the character that is defined through your struggles, and the tenacity that is developed as you embrace the fullness of who you are as a royal Nubian Queen capable of achieving anything to which you put your mind and submit your will. I encourage you to learn your history and your heritage so you can discover the strength, character, and resolve that resonates in your DNA. I leave you with some of my leadership quotes:

"Truth is, some people teach us what to do and some teach us what not to do. Which one are you?"

"Children are adults in seed form. How will you encourage their growth or stunt their growth?"

"Never be afraid or too prideful to use your most basic leadership skills: a hug, a shoulder to cry on, an ear to listen, a hand to hold, simply sitting with someone in silence, a genuine card, a thank you note, a high five, a smile, a prayer, and an encouraging word."

With all my love,

Deneen E. Mosley

...Settle

Dear Beloved Melanin Beauty,

Don't settle for the status quo, or the expectations of others for your life. Burning inside of you are hopes, dreams, and a vision of what you desire to achieve. There will be opposition and challenges in your journey. Those obstacles may come in the form of family, friends, classmates, or acquaintances who have settled and want you to do the same. You may encounter moments of loneliness or being alone, but don't settle! Settling is accepting where you are as your highest or best state or getting comfortable with what you have or what you've achieved. Settle not!

Bless the world with your gifts and talents. Live your life's purpose. It will require a plan and action. You can't impact the world while settling. Yoke up with mentors who will be authentic and transparent, and unafraid to share their challenges. Failing or having experiences that failed does not mean you remain stagnant or sitting. Those events do not define you or your potential.

Beloved, so often society communicates negative personas of us as girls and women. The subliminal message is we should just accept and settle for meager, demeaning relationships and treatment. It is often covertly suggested that we dare not have high expectations, and that we should accept limited access because of our gender and hue. You are the prize! Do not settle!

Honestly examine your life and ask yourself these questions:

1. In what ways have I settled about my dream, vision, and life?
2. Who around me accepts mediocrity, and who expresses power and purpose?
3. When and how will I take a stand against settling?
4. Am I living my life out loud so others can see what not settling looks like?
5. How can I help others take action and not settle?

Embrace all that life has for you, beloved. Settling often leaves you with regrets, disappointments, and failing to realize your fullest potential. Take a step of faith away from the comfort zone of settling. Encircle yourself with a positive cast of people who will not allow you to settle but will be instrumental in propelling you to the next level. You are never too young and never too old to shift from a settled life to a life full of synergy, energy and mobilized for greatness. Shake off the weights. Burdensome associations will keep you from creating encouraging ripple effects of love directed inwardly to yourself and outwardly to others.

Your heart, life, and soul desire and deserve encouragement, empowerment, and elevation. Heal your heart; your soul and life will follow. Ultimately, you will inspire other melanin beauties to cast off the status quo, motivating them to transform their lives from sitting in a position of settling to the action of standing. Maya Angelou said, "Each time a woman stands up for herself, without knowing it possibly, without claiming it, she stands up for all women."

Stand up! Don't Settle!

Peace, joy, and love!

Marilyn Pendelton

Dear Princess Warrior,

Everything you need to accomplish your goals and realize your dreams is within you. That is the one promise I can make to you without reservation. You are strong and powerful and must believe that you never have to settle for anything or anyone. Please hear me when I tell you: Don't settle!

Women are often encouraged to accept what is given to them, or what is expected of them. It is important to know you have choices. You have the ability to set your own course and carve out the path that will lead you to your destiny. It takes preparation, determination, a plan, faith, and an unwavering belief in yourself. There will be challenges and doubters, but you can climb any mountain if you refuse to settle.

What is settling? What does it look like? Settling in your career is when you aspire to be at the top level and someone tells you there is no room for you there, or that you are not talented or smart enough to get there, so you stop trying. You reason with yourself that the level you have reached is fine. Fear and doubt set in and you become comfortable in your discomfort. You ignore the voice in you that says, "You can do this. You are fierce, you are invincible, you are a competitor. This is your race to win!" Instead, you convince yourself that you are happy, doing well, and will one day obtain more. However, when you settle you are never truly happy, you are not really doing that well, and "one day" rarely comes. You silence the voice.

Settling in your relationships is when you go along to get along and become accepting of the unacceptable. You allow someone to treat you in a manner that is less than you deserve, and you start believing your value is based on the other person's interaction with you. You give more of yourself than you receive in return, and you stay quietly unhappy. You keep to yourself and only share the parts of your love life that lead others to believe all is well. Breakaway! People treat you the way you teach them to treat you. Take your life back now!

Do not settle. Instead, I want you to understand the obstacles in your way so you can get over them like an Olympic hurdler. I want you to embrace your Blackness and womanhood as badges of honor—not fade into the darkness of the judgment of others who will not, and cannot, see your capabilities and beauty. I want you to scream "I am here, and I will not go away or cater to your ignorance" to those who label you invisible or try to hide you in their bigotry. I need you to know who you are, be who you are, and love who you are. It is necessary to put settling in the waste pile, and perseverance and self-respect in the recycle bin where they can be used over and over again.

My advice to you may not seem easy but trust me, it is doable. You have the means inside you. You only need to tap into your desires, and the rest is simple. Carry this message to your sisters, so you will continue to hear it yourself. Tell them, don't settle when you are a caterpillar; be still and know that you can sprout your wings and soar as a butterfly. Don't settle when you are a soldier; fight on and claim your place as a warrior.

Love,

Darla M. Character-Johnson

Dear Sister,

You've been in my thoughts. I hope you are doing well. This letter is simply to send you a few encouraging words, and to remind you to keep pressing forward on this journey called life, just in case you feel like settling. It's funny; as little girls we may have had thoughts—even preconceived ideas—about how our life's path would go. Years were planned out, and deadlines set. As I've gotten older, I realize that nobody told me to make room for detours, curve balls, winding roads, missed steps, and stuff beyond my control.

Here's some news: Every event has everything to do with who you are and will shape who you will become. You should know the tapestry of your life was predestined. Before you were born, your entry into this world was stamped in time! You were earmarked with your birthdate, your parents, the level of melanin in your skin, and the circumstances of you. That's how important you are. Down to every finite detail. Your arrival was not a mistake and could not have been more perfectly orchestrated. It all happened according to plan.

You must wonder why I am telling you all of this. I want you to know that, on your best days and your worst days, you matter, and you never have to settle! Unlike a car, you retain your value regardless of the amount of mileage your life has, how often you've moved from one location to another, or having traveled the dirtiest roads. Settling does not have to be your option. Settling denotes sitting or resting in a comfortable position. While that may not be a bad thing occasionally, I encourage you to not settle because you don't believe you deserve better, or because someone told you not to strive for more, or because you made mistakes and now your mind is replaying them back to you. Okay, maybe it's none of the above. Perhaps everything is perfect—and that's the problem. All is well with the world, but you lost your motivation. You can't seem to figure out the next best course of action for you. That's okay.

Every test has an expiration date. There is no reason to settle. Push! Push or pray until something happens for you. It will break. Better days are coming. Life doesn't always go according to plan, and even when it does, sometimes it doesn't yield what we think it should.

Don't let anyone's idea of who you are get mixed up with who you think you should be. Settling and choosing are two different mindsets. You get to do both—or either. The question is: What do you think of yourself? This life affords us many opportunities; we never have to settle on the rung where we've landed. You've been provided just enough light for the step you're on, so take one step at a time.

Loving you to Life!

Alicia L. Littlejohn

Beautiful Black Women and Girls,

There is a popular old saying that goes something like this: If you shoot for the moon, you will at least reach the stars. Basically, this means maximize your potential. Do your best. Strive to reach your goals, and don't settle.

You might be asking yourself, "What does it mean to settle?" It means you have more to offer, more to give, more you're capable of doing—but for whatever reason—you don't try to reach that level of your capability. Sometimes we know we are settling, and other times we don't even realize just how much we have inside of us.

Whether it is emotionally, financially, mentally, physically, romantically, or spiritually; the impact of settling can be felt. I would describe it as a knowing feeling inside; a yearning for more, realizing there has to be something more, but maybe not knowing how to get it. So, we deal with our current situation and dream about things being better but fail to take action towards improvement. A day turns into a week, a week turns into months, and months turn into years. We look back with painful "could, would, and should haves" because we know we chose to settle.

As I write this love letter to you, I speak as a 53-year-old Christian woman who has studied the Bible since the age of nine. I've learned many priceless life principles that have carried me successfully through my life so far. These include: always put God first in all that I do, maintain a connection to community, I am fearfully and wonderfully made, I am to be the head and not the tail, faith can move mountains, God will supply all of my needs, and faith without works is dead. These are just a few of the thousands of scriptures that have positively impacted my life and prevented me from settling for less. I hope these words can bring encouragement to you.

As I close this love letter, I want to encourage you not to give up. Trust that intuitive spirit living inside of you. It is the voice that continues to tell you what you are good at—the gift God has given you. My Bible tells me that your gift will make room for you. That simply means it can take you to unimaginable places and bring you much success in life. That same inner voice tells you the world is bigger than the people around you and to have the courage to go get what you want for your life.

Connect with other like-minded women who have achieved or are striving to achieve a level of excellence in life to support and mentor you. You must be true to yourself. Listen to your voice. Please don't stop dreaming, setting goals, planning, and achieving. You can reach them. It may not be easy, but if it's in you to dream it, it's in you to do it. Please don't settle.

Speaking from love and life experience,

Rita Wells Gorder

To My Dear Sister,

There is always hope.

To settle in life means to take things as they are; to just live life as it comes, doing nothing to change it. You don't have to settle for a mediocre life. You don't have to just live; you can make choices in your life that will help you avoid settling. All aspects of your life can be examined to determine if you are settling. Evaluate your life and identify what is best for you.

There are many areas of life in which you could be settling. Here are a few examples:

We are usually taught to go to school, get a good job, and work for an organization until we retire. To do this is settling, because there are other options. You can be a business owner or try new careers. You don't have to work for someone else or stick to one career, unless that is what you want.

Many people are pressured into certain careers and, even if the career is good, because it's not what they want, they are settling. My advice is to ask yourself questions to analyze what work will be good and fulfilling for you. I know from experience that when you don't follow your passion, it can make you unhappy. Pay attention to what stirs your heart. Examine this, because it is a clue to your passions. Pay attention to your desires. This will help prevent you from settling in a field of work that is not for you.

Another example of settling is in a romantic relationship. Sometimes people are in relationships that are not a good fit. Just like you can analyze what field to work in, you can analyze your relationships. You can weigh the pros and cons, and consider how the person treats you, how they make you feel, and what value they add to your life. Ideally, you'll analyze the relationship before it gets too deep to determine whether the person is right for you.

If you are true to yourself, you will not settle. You will make the choices that are best for you. Yes, it's wise to seek advice and counsel, but always temper that with the knowledge you have of yourself and your desires. You are here for a purpose, and if you don't know the purpose, you will likely settle for less than what your purpose has planned for you. Whatever your passion, follow it because it will lead to a happy and fulfilled life.

We have choices in life, and one is to choose not to settle. Own your life. Figure out what you want. Make the necessary changes. Go get it!

I encourage you, my beautiful sister, to evaluate your life and determine if there are areas in which you may be settling. If that is the case, take steps to change. Choose to win and be a champion. Choose to be successful by not settling.

Remember, there is always hope.

Love,

Noreen N. Henry

Beloved,

Did you know that you are a masterpiece? What if I told you that you are a work of art, created by the ultimate Creator? Would you believe me? If you believe you are a masterpiece, why would you settle for less than what you truly deserve? If you are settling, you must ask yourself some questions, starting with: "What do I need to address in my life that causes me to accept whatever anyone dishes out?" Before we go any further, you should know that what I am about to share with you is something I never said out loud until the beginning of this year. Now, let's continue.

At one point in my life, I realized that a poor self-image dictated much of my life. This revelation came from an epiphany I had at work. I discovered why I stayed involved in a situation long past its expiration date without investigating or heeding the red flags. It was because I wanted to prove to myself and the other party that I am loyal—as loyalty is one of my core values. I had identified a bottleneck in my life and decided to change the narrative, and if I can change my narrative, so can you!

Give yourself permission to survey your life and identify those bottlenecks that have kept you from being great! Now ask yourself, what is holding you back from being your best, living your dream, or simply being the masterpiece that you were created to be? If negative self-talk is filling your head, then I speak life! You are above and not beneath! You are the head, and not the tail! If old ideals are dragging you down, let them go so you can experience freedom! If a poor self-image is making you retreat, learn to love yourself. Loving yourself is a learned behavior, and once you move through the process and get to the other side, we will be waiting for your valuable contribution to the world. Yes, the value proposition that only you can supply! Simply put, you are valuable!

One of my favorite speakers, Les Brown, says it best; "Never let someone else's opinion of you become your reality." Do other people's opinions really matter? The million-dollar question is: What matters to you? Do you believe you are worthy? Do you believe you can have it all? Everyone has a different "all," but consider the basics—which are physical, emotional, mental, and spiritual health. Add the rest of your dreams and goals to your narrative, then ask yourself what's your "all" and can you have it. Figure out what is meaningful to you, and why your best is worth having!

Beloved, there is nothing that should cause you to settle for less than you deserve. In my case, one of my core values was suffocating me. I had to reevaluate what loyalty meant to me, and then turn the page to the next chapter. I hope you never settle for a job, a relationship, a lifestyle, or anything else that doesn't rest well with your spirit. You can change your narrative and change your life. No matter what the situation is or how you got involved, you never have to settle again in this lifetime! You are a masterpiece, and worthy of everything life has to offer you, just as you are!

All the best,

Frankie Roe

Section Four

DO...

...Love Yourself

Dear Queen,

You are loved. You are worthy. You are enough. As you live your life and walk out your purpose, my hope is that you will come to an unconditional love of yourself. A love where you accept your authentic self, all your beauty, flaws, and imperfections. All of you! You are worthy of love. You were created with a purpose; and once you love yourself, you are empowered to do what you were born to do.

For years, I was driven to do more and work harder because I never felt like what I did was enough. If others didn't validate me, who was I to validate myself? It's hard to love yourself when others say negative things about you. Years of verbal abuse weighed on me and kept me from believing I was worthy of love. The few times I let the real me shine; I was met with such negativity I wanted to hide. Maybe you've experienced this yourself? After years of emptying myself for others who took my love, time, and resources for granted, I was fed up. I decided it was time to take care of me and show up for myself and those who I'm called to serve. I wanted to show up authentically, healed, and whole, but first I had to discover the meaning of love and what it meant to love myself.

Loving yourself means doing what is necessary for your emotional, mental, physical, spiritual, and financial well-being. Here are some practical ways you can learn to love yourself:

- Be patient with yourself. Don't be your worst critic. Be mindful of how you speak to yourself. Speak life even when things look the opposite of what you want. Be kind to yourself, and practice self-compassion. Treat yourself the way you would treat someone else going through a difficult time.
- Seek to be a servant. When we are loved, there is something in us that wants to share this amazing experience. We all have things we deal with in

life, but I believe we are blessed to be a blessing. You never know how your actions can help someone else on their journey.

- Practice forgiving yourself. We all make mistakes. When you make a mistake, own it, apologize if you need to, and correct the mistake. Use affirmations. Repeat to yourself every day, "I am loved. I am worthy. I am enough." Do this until you believe it within your inner being.
- Get clear on your priorities. Clarity on your purpose and vision will show you definitively when to say yes, and when to say no. It gives you that extra motivation to persevere when others don't see your vision.

Ultimately Queen, teach others how to love you. Remember, you can only teach others how to love you when you know how to love yourself.

Lovingly,

Mia S. Bradford

To My Beautiful Black Daughter,

The love I have for you is endless. It is not defined by the misconceptions placed on its meaning, but by the pure intentions and actions that I show by writing you this letter. I bring my love to you today with an open heart that beats with the compassion and selflessness I pour into you at this moment. My hope for you as you read this letter is that it speaks to you at the moment you need, and you hear, echoed in my words, this simple phrase: love yourself.

I am not talking about a fairy tale love you read about in books or see on screens in the form of blank faces painted to make you believe that love comes with being hurt and abused. I am talking about the love you show yourself when you wake up every day. The love that others will question when you choose yourself over them. The love you see when you have a rough day, but still find the strength to carry on and walk proudly with a smile on your face. I am talking about love in the form of blessings that the Creator shows you every day in the air you breathe, the sun you feel, and the words you speak.

Love does not look like hurt. Love does not feel like pain. Love does not make you compromise and erase things that make you uniquely who you are. Love is in your smile. Love is in your melanin. Love is your hair. Love is in all of those places that society tells you aren't beautiful on a Black girl. Love is your thoughts, which are spoken through your words that transform into your everyday actions. Love is who you are. You are born and created in love. God didn't place you here without intention. There is a reason for your being. There is a reason for your existence, and I am writing to give you that confirmation.

If no one else speaks these words to you today, tomorrow, next week, next month, or even years from now, just remember, I love you, and I see the love in you. I see it as you are reading this letter. I see it on the days you might not feel your best. I see it when others might feel you haven't done your best. But most importantly, I see the love that you are capable of giving yourself. My beautiful Black daughter, I want you to know that I care. I support you. I share your story with you. When it is all said and done, one thing will remain true: self-love is the greatest gift you can give yourself. Love yourself beyond your circumstances. Love yourself without limitations. Love yourself without self-doubt. No matter what, just keep loving yourself.

All my love,

Marquita L. Allen

My Beautiful Sister,

Allow me to share my story in hopes of inspiring you to make self-care a priority in your life. The phrase "self-care is a form of self-love" sounds cliché, right? I used to think the same thing until August 30, 2017, when my life was forever changed with a diagnosis of breast cancer. Prior to this, I was the modern-day superwoman, much like you I'm sure. I felt the need to do it all. I was a boss with a mid-level management role in a Fortune 100 company, an entrepreneur with a fast-growing business, a loving wife who held down the fort at home, a supportive mother of two young adults, an international traveler, a volunteer for three organizations, and a sister-friend on the scene for every event. Like most superwomen today, I wore my cape with pride and honor, and made it happen! What I didn't know was that a lack of self-care was taking a toll on me mentally, physically and spiritually, and it led to my kryptonite of breast cancer! I learned that chronic illnesses like breast cancer—not to mention mental illnesses like depression and anxiety—can result from a lack of self-care.

What do I mean by self-care? Self-care is the part of self-love that involves you taking care of you. Taking care of you means mindfully and consistently nurturing all aspects of your own well-being; your mind, body and spirit—a *WHOLEistic* approach to vibrant health. It means taking the time to be still, reflect, and rest your body and mind. It means taking the time to prepare and eat foods that nourish your body. It means taking the time to get the exercise your body so desperately needs. It means taking the time to regularly get a good night's rest so that your body can renew itself.

I was blessed through divine intervention to be exposed to holistic medicine, which involved a great deal of self-care. Just like self-care had to become my number one priority to survive, it also has to become yours so you can thrive! What are some things you can do? You can fuel your body by making smarter food choices like eating whole, non-processed foods, getting a full night's rest, and getting at least 30 minutes of body movement a day. You can fuel your mind and spirit by learning to say "no," so you don't overwhelm yourself. Manage the stress in your life through activities like deep breathing and drawing closer to God through prayer and meditation. Go outdoors to connect with nature, do more activities that bring you joy, and address childhood traumas. I had to implement these changes to overcome breast cancer without chemotherapy and radiation. I call these activities the SuperWoman Self-Care System™; where your superpowers come from your ability to love yourself enough to put you first to take control of your health.

Can you relate to being everything to everyone and putting yourself last? I know you can! It's part of our culture—to be the *strong Black woman* and always hold it down no matter what. You won't be of use to anyone if your physical, mental, and spiritual health are suffering. Get self-ish and show self-love with self-care. Your very life depends on it, and your body will thank you for it!

Loving me selfishly,

Nicole Pettiway

Peace and Blessings Beautiful One,

I pray that this letter finds you doing well and in the best of health and spirit. As I write these words to you, I can't help but feel a combination of excitement, joy, and gratitude. To have this unique opportunity to write a love letter to one of the most precious gems on the planet is both an honor and a privilege.

I want to share my heart with you about something very important. It is so important that your world depends on it. Beautiful one, I want to talk to you about love. How perfect that, in my love letter to you, I get the opportunity to talk about love. The type of love I'm talking about is no ordinary love. I'm talking about self-love. One of the world's most beloved artists, Whitney Houston, sang "Learning to love yourself, is the greatest love of all." One reason that self-love is so very important is that it sets the foundation for everything you will ever do and become. Self-love fuels your endeavors and it will impact every relationship you will ever have, including the one with yourself.

Without the proper love for ourselves we can never fully become who God intended, which means we can never reach our full destiny. Self-love is like water; it nourishes our body and gives us life. Can you imagine living without water? Without water, we cannot survive. Without the proper ability to love ourselves, we cannot survive. This four-letter word is critical to our mental, spiritual, emotional, and physical well-being.

Did you know that, if you were to search around the world, you would never find another person on this planet exactly like you? You are uniquely created; from your fingertips to your vocal cords, there is no one else just like you. Only love could have created such a sweet, special, and unique gift to humanity like you.

One reason I thought I would remind you of who you are is that to love ourselves, we must first have the proper understanding and knowledge of ourselves. Love is a principle, that when properly practiced, expressed and understood, can lead to the most divine experiences and produce the most amazing results. Once we embrace the fact that we were all created out of love, it becomes easier to see ourselves from the lens of the one who created us.

If you ever struggle with loving who you are, I want you to remember that you were created from the most supreme kind of love. If you ever doubt how special you are, I want you to look in the mirror at the beautiful reflection staring back at you and embrace what you see. Sometimes we may have to look in that mirror and have a conversation with the person staring back at us. Speak positive words. Speak words that will give life, and help you feel good. Remember, just like the water you so desperately need to survive—you equally need love, self-love.

In sisterhood,

Lakichay Nadira Muhammad

Dear Beautiful Black SLAYdies,

Life does not always go the way we plan. We were taught to go to school, get good grades, go to college, meet the man of our dreams, build a family and long-lasting friendships, retire, and grow old together. I can only imagine what you're thinking, "But what happens when life doesn't go as planned?" I get it! From the time I was a little girl until about 22 years old, I thought I had life all figured and planned out. Sure, I might have to adjust my plans—I was okay with that. But I never thought I'd be 30 years old, single and raising two children, with a good job—but mentally, physically, and financially broken.

For years, I had been abused by people who I loved more than I loved myself. These were people I called friends, family, and lovers. At 16, I spent my spare time with someone who was charming, funny and sweet to most, but was a monster behind closed doors. We physically and verbally fought daily. I didn't realize I had entered a cycle of fighting, forgiving, loving, and staying. Little did I know, this cycle would hold me captive for the next decade of my life and show up in different relationships with the people I loved.

I poured my heart and soul into others and didn't receive that same love back. I had friends and family members I would drop everything for just to make sure they were okay despite what was going on with me. Right before adulthood and parenthood, I began to love a guy who wanted to love the streets and the women in them. But like many women, I got over him by falling for another guy; a man who I spent years loving and fighting. With all the love I gave to others, it never dawned on me I didn't love myself. I couldn't possibly love myself if I accepted the broken, deceptive and abusive love that I received from others.

Are you giving your heart out to the world, and getting nothing in return? Yea, I know how that feels. I've been in love a few times in my life, but never with myself.

I gave so much love and loyalty to others who didn't deserve it and left nothing for myself. No more! How can I expect someone to love me, if I can't love myself? Now, ask yourself that question out loud. Remember, people will treat you how you treat you.

So, to my beautiful, Black SLAYdies, I encourage you to love yourself more! Sometimes as women, we look for love from others instead of giving ourselves the love we want and deserve. Not everyone deserves your love, and not everyone deserves the honor of loving you, especially if they can't love you in a way that honors you. The friends you support and encourage but who only reciprocate with negativity and drama? Let them go! The cousin you tell your secrets to, but she constantly betrays you? Let her go! The guy whose attention and love you have to compete and fight for? Let him go! Honor yourself. Respect yourself. Protect your peace. Start showing people how to love you. Those who want to love you will learn how to love you in the way you need and deserve to be loved.

"A lady who slays in everything she does, is clearly a SLAYdie." Add to the Urban dictionary please!

Jeffonia P. Jones

Dear Past, Present, and Future Me,

You spent years neglecting you, disrespecting you, and taking yourself for granted. Why? You paid more attention to those who had no love for you—entertaining those who had ulterior motives for not liking you or not including you. Their ulterior motives evolved from their fear of your greatness. Even as a child, your greatness was an obvious threat to others. You only wanted to be accepted as yourself. Their plan was to stifle you and cause you to question yourself. The way they felt about you caused you to think you were the problem. With no understanding of your brilliance, your uniqueness was inconceivable to you. With no real knowledge of self, you were conned into not believing in yourself.

You listened to a crowd vested in your downfall and rooting for you to lose. They claimed everything about you was wrong, yet they craved it; wishing you did not have it. Recognizing that you were a diamond, they used group conspiracy to convince you that your exceptionality was wrong. You tried to hide yourself when they rejected you by walking with your head down. The image in the mirror was so convoluted, reflecting the negativity that had been poured into you rather than the beauty that poured from you. Unaware of their plans, you responded to what they said, thinking they were important. It turns out; they were not.

I wish I was there. I would have embraced you so tightly that your insecurities melted away. I would have told you how beautiful and graceful you are. I would have lifted your head so high that you would see past their hate. I would have pulled your shoulders back so your chest would pop with pride in who you already were. Oh, what I would have done had I been there. Thank God, I'm here now!

As a woman, you opened your seemingly blinded eyes as everything began to connect. Your mind, heart, spirit and soul aligned for you to see who you really were. You came into this world alone, and even though that's how it had been since; you learned to be by yourself and to enjoy yourself. You learned that being alone did not equate to being lonely. You learned the difference between desiring company, needing the attention of others, and needing to attend to others. As you came into your own, you realized that loneliness was a state of mind, and that you were complete and whole all by yourself.

Your awakening caused you to see your own beauty, as well as the beauty around you. Courageously, you unpacked the seeds planted in your head that were meant to rob you of your confidence and self-esteem. The pieces of you that were broken and scattered by those who claimed to love you, slowly weaved themselves together again, forming a matrix that made you stronger than you ever were.

Now, you've accepted God's love, and are able to love yourself in the fullness of who you are. Courageously, you've submitted to loving yourself without conditions, restrictions, or limits. You love, without need for confirmation or affirmation, the little girl you were, the woman you are, and the woman you are becoming.

Love,

Dr. LaShonda M. Jackson-Dean

...Love & Be Loved

To My Beautiful Black Business Bestie,

Girl, it's happening again. I'm up at 2:00 am; sweating, heart pounding, wet sheets—and all with my heart on fire and my mind melting. I promised myself that I wouldn't let thoughts of hate, anger, fear, worry, and doubt disrupt my sleep. It's hard enough to keep these emotions from disrupting my day. But you know me, I'm strong! Forget about him. Forget every other man out there. Naw, who am I kidding, girl? That's precisely why I'm angry and twisted right now. It's time to do what my heart is telling me to do. It's time to surrender to love and be open to loving others.

I have not given myself permission to love, and more specifically, to love someone new. I mean, come on; I feel justified in choosing to hate over love. After all, I believe I own the right to hate the man who hated me; who hated me so much that he would share my naked body—my private parts—without my permission with the world. The man who secretly took photos of me while I was asleep, then blasted them onto the Internet. He vowed to silence and destroy me and my 30-year media career and coaching business because I chose to leave him and the controlling, manipulative relationship. While I've since recovered, fought back, won, and now advocate for victims of revenge porn, I still haven't done the one thing I need to do to truly free and liberate myself.

Love.

Love myself enough to forgive him, to love another, and to allow another to love me in return.

I know! How about we do it together? How about we choose to forgive the person or people who wronged us? How about we choose to love ourselves enough to free ourselves from victimhood and hate? How about we choose to open ourselves to loving others so that they may love us in return? How about we choose love together?

I'll offer a few other ways we can choose to love others.

Be present and really listen.
Don't pass judgment.
Set healthy boundaries.
Be spontaneous.
Embrace the good and the bad.
Show unconditional love.

As I lay this pen down, turn over in my bed, and nestle into my pillow; I know I will rest well tonight. I'm choosing the thoughts and energy of love and allowing love to comfort me and usher in a new day and someone new to love.

With love,

Darieth Chisolm

Dear Beautiful Girls,

There are some secrets I want to share with you. The first is that you don't have to be afraid of accepting love. Love is what keeps us going. Let me tell you, so many people love you: your parents (no matter how many times you get into trouble), your grandparents, aunts, uncles, cousins, and especially your friends.

The second secret is that love is like a superpower. Love can make us do anything; it overrides our senses. It can make a person run head-first into danger to help someone they love. It can change someone for the better, taking them off a dark path and helping them find a better one. Telling someone you love them can turn their awful day into a good one.

Love is strong. All those people who love you also support and stand by you. They care for you and have your back. They will boost you and build you up. Their love for you will keep you grounded through the toughest times, even after they're gone.

Love is a complex set of emotions that every human feels. There are different kinds of love, for example; *Storge* is familial love. The type you'd have for a sibling. *Philia* is affectionate love; platonic love you have for a friend. Then there's *Eros*, the romantic kind of love. That leads me to the third secret; there is no need to rush to experience *Eros* love. You'll get there in due time. You can't force yourself to love someone just because you want to be in love—it will make you sick. Romantic love takes maturity and you may not be ready for it yet.

My final secret is that you have to love yourself before you can love others or let them love you. Self-love motivates you to make better and healthier choices in life. It helps you grow as a person, build trust with yourself, stress less, and deal with anxiety. It helps you become more aware of your strengths and weaknesses. And, loving yourself helps you remember that you have value no matter what the media or other people may say. Loving yourself means knowing that you matter. That you belong. You know how to be the best version of yourself; you set the standard for how you allow other people to treat you.

You don't have to be afraid of accepting love, because you deserve it. You are worthy of it. No matter what you do, say or think, you deserve love. You deserve to be loved unconditionally, not because you do something for someone else—but because of who you are. We all need it. We all pursue it. Someone will always care for you and love you. That's a promise.

Love,

Taryn Washington

To my Sister,

I want you to know that you are deserving of love. You deserve to be accepted for who you are. You deserve to be treated with kindness. You deserve to be held in high regard. You deserve to be who you are without fear of ridicule or rejection. I understand that this is often difficult because as women, we often carry so much from our past experiences. I have had tumultuous experiences with love, and I have had a difficult time accepting that I deserved it. The emotional bruises that I suffered throughout my life made it difficult to accept love, and it took a lot of work on myself to help me realize that I was deserving of love.

It was difficult for me to accept love after my divorce. I had built up a wall to protect myself from being hurt again. I didn't know if I could trust someone to really love me and take care of me. In fact, because of the toxic relationship with my ex-husband, I questioned what love was really about.

I offer you some advice: reflect on your journey through life, then identify times when you felt loved. This may be love from a parent, child, or friend. Picture the moment. Where were you? What happened?

What were you wearing? What did it smell like? Get still and imagine yourself back in that moment. Where in your body do you feel the love? Your heart? Your stomach? Your arms? Your legs? Wherever you felt that love, hold on to it as tight as you can. Doesn't that sensation feel good?

We all deserve to feel those sensations and experience love. In fact, without it we cannot survive; it is a basic need. I needed it, and so do you. The more of these experiences you can remember, the easier it will become to challenge yourself and accept the love of others. Not allowing yourself to accept love from another can hurt you. I know that it was stopping me from getting a basic need met and I could feel the effects of it when I went to work, throughout my day, and even when I interacted with my children.

I am not just talking about the love of a significant other. I distanced myself from friends and family members because I was in so much pain. I feared letting others in because I did not want to be judged or appear weak. However, it was during this time in my life when I needed those friends and family the most. I needed their support and guidance. I needed their love.

It takes courage to allow yourself to accept love. You have to be brave enough to risk being hurt. I believe that you can do it. It will require you to release some fears, so take it slow. You will have setbacks but know that it will be worth it because it is what you deserve. Love makes you a stronger person because it enables you to feel support from others. This support will help you get past any obstacles you face.

I share my story in hopes it will encourage you to do the work on yourself and prevent you from allowing things from your past to stop you from accepting love. We all deserve to be loved; however, you must be willing to receive love. We all need love to survive—love for ourselves, and from others.

Love,

Dr. Aubria Nance

My Dearest Soul Sister,

I have been thinking about you. You are an ever-present thought in my mind, so I am taking a moment to tell you that I see you. I understand you. I feel you because I am you. Aesthetically different with our unique fingerprints, yet we are the same. We are viewed by the outside world in similar fashion, fighting an ongoing battle for equality with the core of our being, but that is okay. The battle is not ours and despite the challenges we encounter, I want you to know that no matter what, love others.

I wonder how life's trials and tribulations affect you. How do you handle psychological and physical rejection that inevitably occurs in our lives simply based on our skin tone? Do you stifle the anger that rises from your soul, or do you release it without care, daring anyone to muffle your shout? I have done both; held onto anger to the point where it made me ill and also expressed frustration so loudly, I ruined the image of strength I tried so hard to create. In hindsight, none of that diminishes who I am, and neither will those moments dull your shine. In spite of the who, the when and the why, those lessons were necessary; and what I ultimately learned is the importance of continuing to love others.

Love despite the pain. Love the parent who neglected you; they gave you life. Love the child or sibling who mistreats you or fails to appreciate you; you share a bloodline. Love the partner who hurt you, slighted you, or who made you feel less than; their actions made you stronger. It is not easy, I know. Often, loving others is so very difficult when the feeling is not reciprocated, but during those hurtful experiences is where we discover growth or a lesson we needed to learn. Know that it's okay to love from a distance. Sometimes the hardest thing to accomplish is looking in the mirror to acknowledge and accept the areas in our life where we made the wrong decisions, or where we allowed emotion to guide our actions instead of wisdom. There is growth in the process of healing. Identify the lesson—"the why behind the what"—and move forward. Continue to love no matter what.

Ever find yourself questioning your worth, or doubting your purpose? Admittedly, I've encountered instances where I too have wondered why I wasn't good enough. Why didn't I get that job? Is it the few pounds I need to lose? Is it because I don't "look the part" or maybe I shouldn't have locked my hair? So easy to blame the outside world and harbor resentment when that happens, but life has consistently shown me that I must continue to love. Refuse to allow harsh and unfair judgment to curb your zest for life—for more. I purpose to love, enabling that glow to shine from the inside out. Despite any negativity displayed towards me, my love for others causes my smile to light up a room when I enter. I am undeniably happy with who I am, and the purpose for which I was created.

Bitterness, jealousy, self-doubt, and fear are equal to poisonous darts inserted into the veins of our being. We are so much better and more than the storms we face. Let your love for others be the foundational path that propels you forward. I write this love letter, Soul Sister, to encourage and inspire you to remain unbreakable, unshakable, and unstoppable in establishing your mark in this world. Love on, no matter what.

One love,

Stephanie Lewis

...Help Others

Hey Sis,

I must be honest with you about being in a sisterhood of women. I never thought I would want to be in a sisterhood. I had been hurt so many times by girls and women that I decided "I don't mess with women anymore!" I won't waste my time trying to befriend them, because they are all fake. They cause too much drama; they talk about you behind your back, and they are too messy. Maybe you can relate. You probably have already experienced something like this before. You know, your best friend from school who secretly hated you. Or, the one who you were close to, like sisters, but she despised you because you had a life she wanted.

I know it hurt; I know you felt betrayed, but it was all a setup. They were lessons to teach you about who you are, rather than who they were. I have been there. Associating with people who would hurt you out of the pain you were already experiencing. Being insecure and unsure about things in your life. Not knowing who you are or who you want to be. People-pleasing to get people to like you. Just trying to fit in. The truth is, you'll never fit in trying to be someone you aren't.

I learned this the hard way. At 43 years old, I realized I had no close friends. I prayed for clarity, and the answer was, "you have no close friends because you don't like women." It was a hard truth to face. I didn't like women because I never felt accepted by them. But maybe I never felt accepted because I was busy trying to be who they wanted me to be rather than who I really was.

What I learned from my healing process is a lesson I hope will help you through yours. Women need other women. We are able to create a space for each other that cannot be replicated or duplicated in other types of relationships. A true sisterhood provides non-judgmental care; a place to share openly and get the tools needed to heal and walk in your purpose. But you cannot experience that unless you are willing to provide it for others. Help other women—your sisters—by providing the space to be seen, heard, acknowledged, and validated. You'll find that in doing so, the same space is provided to you. Share your hurts, insecurities, pain, experiences, victories, and losses with other women. Let them know they are not alone. You'll find other sisters willing to share and help you on your journey. Your healing journey can be a beautiful experience that helps you build unbreakable bonds of sisterhood.

If you want to know what true sisterhood looks and feels like, be a sister to another sister. Don't let your past experiences with women or girls keep you from experiencing real sisterhood: love, compassion, support, and honesty from women who choose to call you sister.

We are our sister's keeper,

Latasha Taylor

Dear Beautiful Black Daughter,

You must help others. To help means to be of service by doing or providing something for someone in need. As I live out what I believe to be my true calling, I find myself in the position—in both my personal and professional lives—to give, serve, and love others. I find it only natural to want to pass this on to the next generation. I believe it is important to live a life that leaves a legacy. In an effort to leave a legacy, it is imperative that we help others. When I think of the word help, the following acronym comes to mind:

> Hope
> Empathy
> Love
> Purpose

One benefit of helping others is that it may instill hope or increase hope in self, in life, and in others. Helping others is a remedy to disappointment, despair, and defeat. Helping others may result in giving others hope when they have little to no hope at all. When feeling helpless, one of the best things you can do is help others.

A second benefit of helping others is that it may assist with developing empathy. This is important while attempting to relate to others and their situations when there is a lack of familiarity. Empathy will help you understand how others are feeling, so you may appropriately respond or help the situation. Another benefit of helping others is that it may increase your ability to love yourself and others. There is no greater feeling in the world than love. We all want to love and to be loved. What better way to grow in love than by helping others, by serving others and by giving back? I hope you understand how important it is to help those who are less fortunate through giving back; this is a simple gesture of love.

Helping others may also teach you what your purpose is in life. Having clarity of purpose is important to live your best life. Helping others is important because at some point, we all need help and you can't expect from others what you were never willing to offer. Helping others may allow you to pursue your own priorities. It may also help you prepare for major challenges and overcoming obstacles. Your willingness to help gives value to helping, an understanding of what it means, and the authority to help and serve in love.

Last but not least, my dear beautiful, Black daughter, helping others will help you prepare for the unexpected that comes in life. It will teach you to be resourceful, to approach problem-solving with a passion, and help give meaning to your life.

"People will forget what you said, people will forget what you did, but people will never forget how you made them feel." —Maya Angelou

Love forever,

Melanie Townsend

Dear Beautiful Queens and Princesses,

Do you know one way that can help you elevate and become open to insurmountable blessings? Helping someone else in their time of need, either by thought, word or deed. It is with great joy and reverence that I write to you today on the importance of helping others.

Obedient you. While we all share this universe, our Creator charged us with loving and supporting one another. This is what I hope to do today as you read this letter and I stand in obedience to my purpose. Did you know that being obedient to the Creator sets us up for increase? I am certain that you can use a blessing right now and I want to make sure you know how to obtain one.

Valuable you. As a child, our value system is instilled inside of us by the age of seven. It is my desire that you have a helping nature as the foundation of your basic values. Be kind to that quiet kid with glasses who others seem to look past or pick on. Help the classmate who struggles in the subject you seem to grasp so easily. Be considerate to everyone around you so that, when you become a Queen, people will be fascinated with your energy and want to pour back into you!

Fantastic you. By the time your experiences shape your character, it will be imperative to keep that same helpful aura towards others. Do you know how much better this world will be with you helping all those you can—all those who need you? Whether through a kind word, a thoughtful act or even a smile, you will be a deliberate contributor to someone else's happiness. That by far is one fantastic way to live life.

When you have the spirit to help others, you are blessed ten times over. If you can empower, enlighten, and encourage someone else to be their best version of themselves, you've just created an impactful legacy to the world. Empower, enlighten, and encourage; this is the 3E method I developed, and now teach to my clients who are professional women.

When you take time to encourage others in their time of need, you change the trajectory of their lives. When you become an adult, don't forget this amazing trait of helping others, and carry that with you always, in both professional and personal goals.

I send you love when you're discouraged. I send you peace when you're confused. I send you happiness when you are unmotivated and sad.

I hope that you dream big! I hope that you love bigger! I hope that, in your helping others you become your best self. There is no comparison to the joy and fulfilment obtained when you're able to help improve someone else's life. Even when you're down, it costs nothing to assist in uplifting our fellow human beings. The affirmations and possibilities are endless, and the reward is great. Helping others is our duty, and I want you to be the best!

Lovingly,

Dawn M. Perry

Dearest Darling,

I write this letter to you as a reminder—in case you ever get caught up with someone or something that makes you question your purpose, your value or your worth. I'm here to tell you that you are absolutely wonderful, and you matter, just as you are. As a matter of fact, just know that you are a unique, one-of-a-kind miracle created by God. There is no one in the world made quite like you, and no one is as good at being you, as you are. You would only fail if you tried being someone you are not.

Who you are matters for many reasons; one of which is that you were specifically placed on the planet—right here, right now—to make a difference in this time. Being you means that you have a unique perspective. No one else has your perspective, that is why you must make a difference. You were put here in this world to change it, tweak it and make it better. We need you to add your unique mix of ingredients (your perspective, ideas, talents, and your determination) to each and every situation you encounter for a purpose.

You see, the things you think and say always have a level of impact beyond just yourself. You are part of a larger community. Pay attention to the choices you make with your thoughts, spoken words, and actions. They change things. They change things for others and for you.

Sometimes people blame others for what they say and do but I assure you, you always have a choice. It may require being willing to think your way through a situation instead of feeling your way through—but you always have a choice. Please remember that. You are responsible for what you say and do.

When you choose to carefully consider what will happen after your next move, you can choose the best move to make. You will have either a positive, neutral, or negative impact on every situation you encounter. Consider that when you approach situations that teeter on the line of good or bad. Your voice, your action, or even your intentions can sway things one way or the other. Pick the positive. Choose the better one.

Mother used to say, "Baby, the room should be better after you leave it than when you first came in." She wanted me to remember that when I am added to a situation; that situation should somehow be better than before I showed up. That's because I was to choose to make it better. Now, you might be asking why you have to be so careful when others are not, and why you have to be thoughtful when so many others are not. As I learned from a very wise woman, Dr. Johnnetta Cole, the reason I have to give, give, and give towards making the world a better place is because there has to be balance in the world. There are so many who make neutral or negative impact choices, that more of us must make the positive ones.

Honey, be a positive influence. Make the world better. Bring yourself to every table, and let your voice be heard. There is only one you. Be that, and the world will be a better place because of you.

I love you,

Dr. Torri Love Griffin

Hey Sis,

If you are like me, you grew up feeling obligated to make this world a better place for those who come after you. And, if you are like me, you've probably felt that you are not seen or accepted for who you really are. You and I spent a lot of time trying to adapt and make ourselves more palatable for others because who we are is not acceptable. Yet, you believe if one of us is not free, none of us are free. With all of these messages in our heads, we often place value on making a difference in order to be better. I encourage you to become better in order to make a greater difference. This takes commitment to our authentic selves, and to service. The greatest difference you will make will be after you have breakthroughs in your thinking and your actions. Only after those shifts, will you reach more people and make a greater difference in their lives.

Sis, I spent many years mothering other people's children. I wanted to care for them in ways that were meaningful to them, not just meaningful for me. It is soul-fulfilling to serve people in ways that mean something to them. I did not always do that well; that came from having personal breakthroughs. I have seen a lot of Black women miss making a real difference because they keep struggling to be seen or accepted by someone else's standards.

Several years ago, I had a breakthrough around my own privilege. We were just making strides to legally meet the needs of the gay community in the state where I lived. Before this, I did not understand my heterosexual privilege. Once I finally understood that I could marry, share healthcare benefits, and even sit by the deathbed of the love of my life; I realized that I had privileges some were not given. Once I got that, I realized how some white folks don't get racism. Wow!

That breakthrough helped me understand other people's blind spots and caused a permanent shift in my thinking. It softened my hard heart around racism and people with racial privilege. Not only was I less angry, I could look into the eyes of a white person who I wasn't close to and see a person who "wasn't aware of what they didn't know," like me. From that point on, more white folks could receive transformation through me, and it keeps happening decades later. I became better at connecting because I could relate to not knowing and needing the grace I had learned to give others. As I grew and stood up for vulnerable people—even when I was not palatable—I made the greatest difference and experienced the most joy being myself because of it.

Please have courage to be your authentic self. You will be the difference you want to see as you serve others. Enjoy the Journey.

Love,

Rochelle Peterson-Ansari

Dear Sis,

If you were born into a broken family, voted less likely to succeed, and never thought you would be anything, then I'm writing this letter to you. I am you. You are me. We are one.

I wasn't voted the homecoming queen. I considered myself the ugly duckling of the family and never thought very highly of myself for a long time. Thinking that way about myself led me to make decisions early in life that caused me a lot of pain. Sis, can you relate?

I was awakened to the fact I was born to make a difference and my life changed forever. I hope wherever this letter finds you today that it also awakens you to that fact in your life. I want you to know that I believe in you. I believe in your dreams. I believe in your goals. I know you have them because everyone placed here by the Most High has a specific assignment to carry out. You have a purpose sis, and it's not too late or even too early for you to start the journey. Someone is counting on you to walk it out!

I want you to know that you were born for such a time as this, and you were called to make a difference. In the book of Jeremiah (1:5 NIV), it says that God knew us before we were in our mother's womb. That means even before conception, there was a purpose for your arrival; a purpose that only you can fulfill. We need you, sis.

I cannot ignore the fact that for many of us life has been extremely hard. We've had to be the best at everything we do. Then when we do our best, we are told it's not good enough. This would exhaust anyone, but don't give up my sister.

I want you to know, despite everything that has happened in your life or that may happen, you have what it takes to be great. There is nobody like you in this entire world. Your fingerprint—and everything about you—is unique. Only you can do what you were born to do; and I want you to know, Black woman, you are amazing. Sis, this world needs you now more than ever. Our children need your presence. We need you to do your part in this world. We need you to stand up and be counted. Leave an impact that cannot be forgotten.

It's not the time for you to shrink back and hide. It's time for you to stand up. It's time for you to tell your story. It's time for you to tell your truth. We won't judge you, sis. We won't talk about you behind your back. We are going to love you. We are going to appreciate you.

It's time, dear sister, for you to rise up and make a difference. The world is waiting on you—the authentic you. Nobody else can do what you were born to do. No one can fulfill the assignment you were put here to complete. It's your time, and it's your turn.

Love,

Keysha Bass

My Sister, My Friend, I Celebrate You!

You have the power to make a change and be the difference.

When I was younger, I wanted to be like so many other people. Dress like the top model, wear my hair in all the new trends, talk, rap, and sing like the latest star. I was walking, talking and looking the part. I had been studying the role so closely; I knew all the lines by heart. Finally, I was accepted by all the "cool" people who had it going on. Just when I thought I had everything right, the script changed, and I had to learn new lines. New hairstyles, new sneakers, new dance steps, new wardrobes—everything new again and again. I was driving myself crazy!

I remember one day so clearly, feeling like I didn't fit in anywhere. Not at home, school, church, or in my community. Maybe you can relate? Feeling anxious, confused, hurt and lonely. You see, you can only pretend to be someone you are not for so long. My grandmother was the only one around me who was attuned to my emotions and asked me what was wrong. After I explained what was wrong, she shared some things that helped change my perception of who I was and, as a result, my trajectory in life.

After running down a long list of positive traits, qualities, and skills she saw in me, I was even more confused. Then she told me I was spending so much time learning someone else's lifestyle, mannerisms, and experiences that I couldn't see the value in my life. She encouraged me to spend more time learning who I was and writing my own script.

The moral of the story is to stop trying to find yourself and your validation in other people. You have the ability and strength inside of you to be a changemaker. Spend time finding out who that person is. Once you find that person, you are no longer the carbon copy; you are the original who others will try to copy. Your situation does not determine your destiny; your choices determine your destiny. You; the quirky you, the imperfect you, the confused you, the smart you, the insecure you, and the "got it all together" you—everything you need for the difference you are called to make in this world is inside of you.

If it's a cure for cancer, it's in you.
If it's breaking generational curses, it's in you.
If it's a cure for multiple sclerosis, it's in you.

In you is the ability to tell your story and save someone's life. In you is the change needed for a better home life. In you is the power to create a better community. In you is the leadership needed for a better state. In you is the ability to make this a better world.

Inside of you is a better you; a better mother, a better sister, a better aunt, a better cousin, and a better friend. In you is the ability to be a changemaker!

Go change the world!

Charlotte Miller-Lacy

Dear Beautiful Black Girl,

You were not called to be stationary in this life. You have been called to a mission. Your mission is to make a difference in the world. Your mission is to use the gifts you were born with to make the world a better place. Your mission is to be fulfilled. You can't wait on others to give you permission to make a difference. You can't wait for others to define your path. You must stand up and be a voice for others who can't speak. The time is now. You are not meant to stand still. You must realize that making a difference is your divine assignment.

You can make a difference in the world by being a vehicle for change. Your career path is that vehicle. Whatever career path you choose, it's a tool to improve someone's life. Use your gifts, strengths, and power to bring change to your community. Use your education, knowledge, and experience to resolve inequality, combat crime, and battle social injustice. Use your expertise as a tool to bring economic empowerment, political power, and systemic change. Without you, the world cannot succeed. Without you, another little Black girl may never see change. Without you, the mission will not be accomplished.

Everyone is not called for this mission, but you are. You were meant to be an advocate, a leader and change agent. There are people waiting on you to speak up. There are people waiting on you to take action. There are people waiting on you to be the voice of change. Change is never easy. In fact, you will be met with resistance. There will be some people who won't understand your mission. There will be roadblocks on your journey. The key to overcoming these roadblocks is to stay steadfast and be committed to making a difference. Remember your calling and your purpose. Think about the leaders in history who met with resistance. Think about how committed they were to their cause. Think about all the sacrifices they made to make a difference. Your journey won't be any different, but it will be worth it in the end.

Lastly, I want you to understand that while making a difference, you must also leave a legacy for others to follow. You must create a path and stepping-stone for other Black girls coming after you. The legacy you leave for others is important because it sets the stage for what others will do. It's important for you to understand that others will remember what you do. Others will look at the work, the sacrifice, and leadership you left behind. Your legacy is less about individual fame, but the impact of your work. Your legacy is about leaving the world better than you found it. It is up to you to fulfill your mission. It is up to you to make a difference. We are depending on you.

All my love and success,

Jinnell Killingsworth

To My Beautiful Young Queen,

We are the shoulders on which you, our future, stand.

These words spring from the sisterhood of women who, over the years, have become our extended family. To me, it is such a profound statement because it expresses the impact we have on the future simply by being who we are—completely and unapologetically. We have a responsibility to you; to do good because it is right, and to do what is right because it is good. I hope my love and guidance gives you the tools you need to build that future.

Now is the time to reconnect with our divine history, recognizing that we were a powerful civilization before we were discovered, and to reject slavery as our dominant narrative. Now is the time to restore our feminine power, recover our magic, and realize that Black girls do, in no uncertain terms, rock. Now is the time to renew our efforts and remember that we are descendants of kings and queens and therefore have inherited a lineage that is not written in textbooks, but rather lives in our spirit. Royalty is our birthright. Encoded within us is everything we need to reach the fullest manifestation of who we are destined to become.

Oprah reminds us to, "Think like a queen," and goes on to say that "a queen is not afraid to fail. Failure is another stepping-stone to greatness." Do not be afraid to claim your royal legacy and be the queen you are destined to be. We have the power to affect positive change just by our presence. Queens are meant to lead. We can build nations, and we can move mountains. We are phenomenal women.

Your vibrant energy shines like a beautiful gem in your crown. I want to encourage you to find your passion and embrace your purpose. Persevere on your journey with your head held high, knowing that you have our shoulders to support you in making a difference in the world. Never give up. Share your gifts and talents in remarkable ways that build our communities and empower others. Shine, young queen! Be a light for others and help them see the light in themselves.

Together we are stronger, our voices are louder, and the synergy of our actions more powerful. What you are capable of achieving is only limited by your imagination. You are strong and amazing; and I am so very proud of the determined young lady you've become. I know you can do whatever you set your mind to, and I also know you will leave an indelible mark on this earth. Be caring. Be kind. Be generous. But most of all, be yourself.

Remember to leave the world a better place than you found it, and someday, you will be the shoulders on which tomorrow's future will stand.

Love,

Dr. Nathalie C. Lilavois

...Stand Tall

Dearest and Sweetest You,

It took a moment before I could find you in the crowd. You burrowed yourself deep within the mediocrity, shielding your light behind others who did not shine as brightly as you. I saw the light from where I was standing, emanating from you, colors as bright as the sun. I noticed you shy away from the natural spotlight that so graciously followed you so you could blend in with the others. I saw you purposely dulling your shine.

I am writing this letter because I resonated with your desire to be unseen. I too lived an existence where it was easier to dim my light than it was to fully embrace my power. You see, I had something burning inside of me. I had something filled with so much veracity that it made me sweat every time I opened my mouth to say a word. It paralyzed me with fear every time I imagined how others would look at me when I finally gave in to my strengths and revealed my power. It scared me to be different; it terrified me to be identified as something unique. I preferred the comfort of shrinking myself, but I had no choice than to finally embrace the fullness of my abilities and stand tall.

Often, we convince ourselves that we must conform to be accepted. We don't want others to perceive us as "doing too much," knowing too much, or thinking we are "all that." I am here to let you know that it is okay to do too much, if you don't exhaust yourself doing so. It is okay to know too much, because knowing just enough will never be enough. And, please think you are more than all that because you are. You are the greatest version of you ever created. You have been equipped with gifts that you must share with the world. It is your birthright to let your light be a beacon. Your light will not blind the people vibrating on your frequency. They will be drawn to it like moths to a flame. They will have no choice but to accept the gifts you lay down before them. You are not meant to kneel behind the masses. Stand tall.

The people who are meant to find you will always find you, but you must stand tall in case they aren't standing tall enough to see you yet. You must remove the obstructions from their views by standing upright. Fully, boldly and unapologetically on your foundation and principle, you must stand tall. I'll be here waiting to bask in your light.

Standing tall right beside you,

F. Renee Hamilton

To the Courageous Black Girls Leading Us Through the 21st Century and Beyond,

You are beautiful. There is so much power in your being that you might not realize. I know, sometimes it's difficult—being a Black girl, that is. I think it's because people are overwhelmed with our beauty; and when we walk into a room, they see our potential and power beaming from us, and that intimidates others. Is it tough watching TV or scrolling through social media and not seeing a lot of people who look like you? Yes. But never let that knock you down. Strive to be the lead role in your favorite TV show; let everyone see what a Black girl can really do—she can do everything.

You can be the lead scientist on a big experiment; you can own your own business, write your own book, or become a deep-sea diver. You can do anything. When people try to put you in a corner or make you think you aren't meant for these roles, make them see why you should be doing the job, or playing the role. Stand firm in what you believe to be true, because for too long people have tried to break us down and make us feel like we don't deserve an equal shot—but we do. One of the biggest, most essential things for us Black girls to learn is how to use our voices. You, beautiful Black girl, have one of the strongest, most valid voices out there—so never hesitate to speak up. Not only do you have the support of every Black girl around you—you also have the support of every Black girl who came before you.

It is important to look back and remember the hard work and dedication so many Black women put forward so that today we can live better, more equitable lives. There is still a ton of work to do, and you can do it! Now, this does not mean you need to lead a protest or become a public speaker; you can use your voice through your everyday actions. This could be on the playground, at your sports practice, at a sleepover, or in the lunchroom. Your voice is extraordinary and needed at every single one of these places. There is a lot of injustice in this world, and it is our generation that can break through it. We can make people feel the power in our voices, and the power of the voices that were silenced before us. The most crucial thing they should know about us, is that we always stand tall. We stand tall even when it seems like we stand alone, but it is imperative to know that you are never—and I mean never—standing alone. You will always have me and many other Black girls standing in your corner.

Read this aloud: I am strong. I am mighty. I am steadfast. I am immovable. There is nothing that I cannot do if I keep the faith.

Love,

Savannah Shepherd

My Dear Melanin Sister,

I love you; I love you; I love you! I am so grateful for this opportunity to send you a piece of my heart. It is my desire that you know just how special and unique you are. I am writing to encourage you to stand tall in the power of who you are.

On your journey, you will meet good and bad people, and experience good and bad situations. At times, you'll be amazed, and other times you may be left traumatized. It is during the worst of times and with the worst of people when you must reach inside to find the strength to make it through and stand tall in the midst of it all.

Know this my sister; standing tall does not mean that you must carry the burden yourself. It means that you walk boldly and courageously through life, and its circumstances. It means that if you need help, you find the strength to ask for it. If you need to cry, find the strength to be vulnerable. If you need to make a dramatic change, find the strength to make it. Your ability to operate in the power within you can be your doorway towards healing and success.

So, my dear sister, when life's ups and downs come your way, hold on to that inner strength and stand tall despite outside influences that try to rob you of your joy. Don't compare yourself or your experiences to anyone else's. Own your life. Love your life. Own the experiences you've had; and own the person you've become because of those experiences. Despite it all, you are still special and unique. Stand tall when you enter the room. Look up. Be confident.

I want you to learn to encourage yourself, my sister. Know that your belief in yourself is the only thing you really need to survive and thrive in this life. Experiences may knock you down, but it is your belief in yourself and your ability to recover that will enable you to rise again. Always find your way back to yourself.

I want you to know your success is expected and needed. Someone is looking to you for guidance on how to make their way in this world. So, stand tall and stand strong. Show them how it's done.

I hope my words reach the deepest part of your heart and ignites your hope. Stand tall, my sister!

Remember, I love you!

Mary Hazward Fernandez

My Fellow Teenage Mother,

Rumors are being spread; you're feeling lost and confused about a decision that you must make. Too young to understand all of what's happening in your life with the life that's now growing inside of you.

I see that you're afraid to tell anyone, but the swelling of your belly can no longer be hidden. I get it, you're in a sticky situation and afraid to talk to your mother or father with the fear of being punished for something to which they contributed.

You didn't want to find love in a man, but the love at home was not something you could understand. You watched your mother and father argue, fuss, and fight and that led you into the arms of what felt good to you inside. Creating a life was not something you expected to happen because you were too young to understand what might really happen. He was everything you wanted and needed to feel good about yourself; and at your tender age, it was more than what you were getting and needed at home.

So, what is a young teenage girl to do? You are just a baby yourself with a baby growing inside of you. Decisions, decisions, decisions! Not a good place to be in at your age and underdeveloped mindset. There is so much yet to explore in this life; but for now, all you know is that the life ahead of you is unknown.

You finally get brave enough to face the world and decide that you're going to have this beautiful new baby. It's okay, my child, you're not alone. So many others just like you have had babies while still being a baby, and still conquered the world. On the day of your delivery, some may come to be with you to welcome this new bundle of joy. Surprisingly, you may find yourself filled with so much happiness.

Now the reality of life kicks in and you're a teen mom wondering what's out here for you in this world. All your peers are having fun, going out, and partying with their friends. You're thinking that it is not fair and wondering how you can turn back time. That time before you opened yourself to adulthood too soon. It's true that you must grow up a lot faster than everyone else around you now and realize, sooner than later, that life is not all fun and games. You can't just mess up like many teenagers do because you have another life that depends on you.

Here is the golden nugget of this life lesson you will realize: Once you embrace your responsibility of being a mother, you will have something to work hard for in this life, and someone to make proud. Life is not over by a long shot. Keep your head up and reach for the stars. I promise you; you got this! You have much to offer to so many others who will walk in your shoes. When you're going through life's ups and downs (which is a process for us all), always remember to stand tall!

I'm here for you.

Truly,

Angelita Byrd

Sister,

Let's face it. We all make mistakes and have been impacted personally by the unexpected that resulted in loss, disappointment, or defeat. We've come up against challenging situations that made us feel uncomfortable, people (sometimes the ones closest to us) who made us feel less than, and that our opinions or contributions don't have value. Some of us had our ideas or proposals challenged and minimized in professional settings not because of its content, but because of our gender, or color of our skin. In these situations, we got knocked down, and it hurt. We lost our confidence, and we wanted to run and hide—to give up. You will get pushed and gut-punched throughout life. The question we must ask ourselves when this happens is whether we will stand down or stand tall.

Do you recognize what it feels like to stand down? Standing down is believing what people say about you and allowing those negative thoughts and perceptions to consume your mind, influence your thinking, and dictate your actions. If this is you, then please stop immediately. It is holding you back from achieving greatness. Stand tall!

Standing down is also not owning the part you play; always thinking it's everyone else's fault or that you are the victim. I know you're probably thinking, "You don't understand what they did!" Or, "Why me?"

Breathe, take a step back, and look at the entire situation (not just how you feel) to see all sides, reflect on how things could have been done differently to achieve a better outcome, and how you can grow from the experience. I get it; inward reflection and taking the necessary steps to own your actions is tough, but it's necessary as we journey through life. Do the work. It will be worth it. Stand tall!

Finally, standing down is when you think you can't overcome the unmerited opinions that influence your reputation and professional success. It's when you either give up or succumb to the pressures in school or the workplace, allowing others to get in your head, and eventually impact or limit your performance. Don't give those people the power to control your life. You are destined for greatness, you can do all things; and no matter what, you deserve to own your opinions, thoughts and ideas, and have the same opportunities to showcase your talents so you can "level up" and thrive. Stand tall!

Standing tall starts with being honest with yourself and the situation. It takes courage, hard work, confidence, inward and outward strength under pressure and to be intentional in all aspects of your life. You have to believe in yourself; be humble—but never let your haters see you sweat. Effectively influence and respectfully own your ideas and get the help you need to have a strong and sound peace of mind. It means that you plan your work and work your plan, and you do not give up until your desired results are achieved. Stand tall!

Sis, the only person stopping you from achieving greatness and being all that you can be is you. Have faith in your hopes and dreams, then get out of your own way and get to work. I believe in you. You've got this! So, when you feel you want to stand down, Stand tall!

Love ya,

Dana M. Harris

...Celebrate Yourself

My Dear Divine Queen,

I'm taking a moment to tell you that now is the time to celebrate yourself! Life will always be full of ups, downs, and in betweens; but through it all, celebrate you! It is most important to reward yourself during those moments when life seems like it's beating you down. You suffered a major loss, such as a job. Your significant other left you. You failed a class. You're behind on bills. You received some bad news about your health or the passing of a loved one. Yet you still managed to shower, feed the kids, and answer a call from a friend who needed you to put on a smile—when all you wanted to do was cry. Guess what! You deserve to be celebrated.

There isn't always a perfect time to pop the champagne, eat off the good china, have a girls' night, or wear that red lipstick, so you have to create the occasions for yourself. You are divine in your own right. Through the wins and losses, there are lessons learned. And if you don't recognize yourself as the Queen you are, who will? You are the entire Universe in human form. You radiate the same energy and light as the sun. The power of the ocean's waves roar within you. Recognizing these traits alone will place jewels in your crown! As women, we have the power to command attention by just being present. When we realize this and celebrate our magnificence, everyone else will have no choice but to follow suit. Our time on this earth is not promised from one day to the next; we witness that daily. Lives are lost within a blink of an eye; therefore, I implore you to not wait for that raise to pay on a trip or wait to meet your soulmate before you set your alarm to watch a breathtaking sunrise. Don't wait until you become a mother to find joy and laughter in the little things. Now is the time! Who says there has to be a limit on how often you uplift yourself?

Please, the next time you pass a mirror, I want you to stop and gaze upon yourself as one of God's greatest creations, and pat your fro, flip those coils, shake those curls, swing those locs or caress that beautiful bald head. Smile and say, "I celebrate the Queen that I am because I have been through some things and I am not broken, even if I am bruised. I am a marvelous work in progress, and bruises heal. As long as I have air in my lungs and two feet above ground, I will celebrate me; unapologetically!"

Finally, I will leave you with a quote from Stephanie Lahart: "You are original, unique, and exquisite! Embrace your imperfections with confidence and self-love. Your authentic self is your best self! Flaws and all, you are still a rare gem! Black woman, you are phenomenal, please believe that!"

Loving you royally,

Angel Morgan

Dear Sister,

Celebrate yourself! Why? Because you are a unique and magical woman. There has never been and will never again be a woman like you. You, my sister, are worthy of celebration. As Black women, we are rarely taught to celebrate ourselves; in fact, we may be led to believe the opposite—that we are not worthy of celebration. We are more likely to celebrate others than take the time to celebrate ourselves. Celebration of self is not a luxury. It is a necessity that makes us better equipped to be friends, sisters, mothers and daughters while also being our best selves.

Loving yourself is a way to celebrate you. Every day when you rise and look at yourself in the mirror, smile at that gorgeous creature. Marvel in the beauty of her hair, the glow in her eyes, every dip and curve of her body. She is your temple. Accept her as she is—glories and faults—and love her for the rest of her days as only you can. Celebrate yourself by loving you.

Respecting yourself is a way to celebrate you. You respect yourself by living well and taking care of your body. You respect yourself by demanding that others treat you respectfully, whether by their words or actions. People treat valuable items with respect. You are as valuable as any other treasure. Celebrate yourself by always respecting yourself and expecting to be respected.

Practicing self-care is a way to celebrate you. Black women tend to overlook self-care because we focus more on giving ourselves to others. Celebrating yourself by practicing self-care will enable you to feel your best, restore your energy, and allow you to have the reserves you need to live your best life and bless others. Never feel guilty or ashamed for taking care of you! Take walks in the sunshine, curl up with a good book, give yourself a manicure, or spend time on your passion project. Celebrate yourself by prioritizing self-care.

Surround yourself in positivity. Be an optimist and expect the best for yourself. Be grateful for what you have, for what you can do, and for who you have in your life. Learn how to be grateful for what you thought you wanted that did not come to pass. Celebrate the disappointments that turned out to be blessings in disguise. Approaching life with a positive attitude and a spirit of gratefulness will make it easier to see all there is to celebrate in your life.

Celebrate you by pouring some of your magic into your sister. It does not matter if it is your blood sister, your sister-friend, or a stranger on the street. Celebrate you by sharing your talents, your wisdom, your friendship, and your love with your sisters. Set an example by proudly celebrating yourself every day.

Remember, there has never been and never will again be a woman like you. So, why not celebrate? You and all of our sisters are more than worthy.

Cheers!

Tina C. Powers

Dear Sister,

Who doesn't need a cheerleader rooting them on? For as long as I can remember, my mom has been my biggest cheerleader, champion, advocate, and fan. In her eyes, I am fearless, capable, and talented enough to achieve anything I set out to do. As I think back to the plays I participated in with no real acting skills and the cheerleading tryouts (which I didn't make), my mom was constantly shouting, "You can do it!" From my highest moments to my lowest, she has been the rock in my corner; encouraging me to be better, chase my dreams, tune out the haters, and achieve my God-given talent. Just as my mother planted those seeds of greatness in me, I imparted the same in my daughter, as she will in hers someday.

As I got older, my village expanded to include aunts, cousins, colleagues, and my absolute favorite girlfriends. There is only one guarantee in life: you will experience peaks and valleys in your time. Prayerfully, your good days will far outweigh the bad; but regardless of the curves, take time to celebrate you and the women and girls in your life. Trust me, you are going to need your village coaching you, praying with you, and cheering for you. Here are a few lessons learned in my journey.

People matter. Developing genuine, authentic relationships is key. Surround yourself with girlfriends who are evenly yoked, positive, and who inspire you. At times, you may give your best, and still people may mistreat you. But your inner circle—those who love you and have your best interest at heart—will rally with you. Your village will cover and protect you, even when you are not aware that they are. I know this from my experience. So, keep the faith, and don't ever grow weary of doing good. Be your own champion. It is great to have a village celebrating with you but learn to be your own champion and speak to yourself with daily affirmations. "I am amazing." "I am more than a conqueror." "I can do anything I put my mind to." "I've got this." Leverage your village to echo these sentiments to reaffirm that you are talented, smart, and a winner.

Have grit. Always show up and give one hundred percent. Hard work takes commitment and determination. Surround yourself with people who have the same work ethic. Stop, pause, and celebrate along the way. Root for yourself and others with the same tenacity and passion.

Be resilient. Don't let adversity stop you from achieving your goals. Whatever the barrier, join forces with your village to find ways to go over, around, or through the barriers. When you do, celebrate these moments. Small victories. Big wins. Either way, can you say, "party?"

Last but not least, make your village your foundation, safety net, and biggest champion. Within your village, there is always unconditional love and support and a non-judgmental protective space where you can be you. You are standing on the shoulders of some amazing women who want you to soar. Dance, laugh, play, and above all, love. Love your community, love your village, and love the woman you are and the woman you will become, and never stop celebrating with your village.

Your biggest cheerleader,

Michelle A. Taylor

Greetings Agent Beautiful,

It has been brought to my attention that you may be deficient in one of the mandatory assignments given to you. You were presented with this task because after conducting several extensive searches, which all ended in negative results, you are the only one qualified to complete such a task. Know that others will try and have tried; others have even come close, but this assignment has your name written all over it; and I know with great confidence you can do it with 100% success. I hope you're not getting scared or feeling pressured. As I type these words, I am filled with so much joy, because I know that once you understand the assignment, you are going to give it your all. That is how much I believe in you.

Once I have detailed the assignment, I need you to approach it with great urgency and importance. Listed below is your assignment. After reading this letter, immediate remedies, action plans, consistency, and commitment are needed. This information can and should be disseminated to as many Black women and girls as possible. Though I have not given you a guideline on how this must be accomplished, I trust that you will tailor it to fit your life for guaranteed success. Are you ready to accept your assignment, Agent Beautiful?

Assignment: Celebrate Yourself

Never go a day without acknowledging yourself and your accomplishments. Even if it's something small, something so everyday(ish) or something others don't see or consider being something to celebrate, celebrate yourself. Nobody has to know, give approval, permission or share their thoughts and opinions about how you love and celebrate yourself.

It does not always have to be a grand gesture or cost you something. Affirm yourself. Pat yourself on the back. Indulge in your favorite snack. Dance. Sing. Tell yourself that you are the truth! But occasionally, go all out for yourself. Spend the money. Take the trip. Buy the shoes. Lavish yourself in luxury. You deserve it—trust me—you deserve it!

Recognize what's worth celebrating. You opened your eyes this morning; celebrate your life! You chose to walk away when you had every right to snap; celebrate your maturity. You completed a project; celebrate a job well done. You survived a difficult period in your life; celebrate your resiliency and strength.

Find opportunities to celebrate yourself. When those opportunities are few and far between, celebrate the lessons you learn on your way to the next celebration. Don't wait for others to celebrate you or acknowledge your greatness. Their validation is not evidence of your worthiness. You deserve to be celebrated every day. So, Agent Beautiful, as you begin this mission, I look forward to seeing how you grow and shine as you recognize how wonderful you are. Thanks for being on the team and doing your part!

With love and respect,

Tam Watkins

Dear Strong, Beautiful, Boisterous, Bold, Smart & Vivacious Daughters,

You are a precious body of flesh, who deserves all that life has to offer. Make yourself a priority and celebrate yourself in all facets of life. You deserve to live, love, and laugh. My purpose for this letter is to advise you to always celebrate yourself and your life's journey. Even when life gives you lemons, make lemonade, then toast and celebrate you!

In my early twenties, I experienced verbal and physical abuse at the hands of my children's father. My life changed without notice, and I became a single parent. I only had a high school diploma, and no work experience. I was often sad and felt depressed, but I had to figure out how to adapt to the situation. I had to change my mindset, realize that it was not okay to be abused, and renew myself for the sake of my children. This is when I figured out that if I didn't put myself and my kids first, it would never end. I needed to be strong and believe life was better than being abused. I also knew that I was destined to be more than a "baby mama" who was abused. I felt like giving up and letting go, but I couldn't because I had two little girls depending on me. Life was unfair, and it was not their fault; so, I learned to lean on what I knew to see me through. This was not my life to destroy, so I was forced to make unwanted changes, and experienced pain in doing so. I rebounded from that period of my life, but I didn't do it alone. I did it with family, friends, prayer, and love. I learned that celebrating allowed me to reflect on my healing process, learn to love myself again, and accept my difficulties. I also learned to celebrate myself through all of life's obstacles.

Make a habit of celebrating yourself even through life's disappointments, promotions, celebrations, and just because. Celebration does not always mean a party; it could be a pair of expensive shoes, a new bag, dinner, or something just for you! Celebrating is a way to forget what you have been through, or something to do simply because you are happy. Celebrating is what I did to heal from the pain. I was hiding and did not always want people to know what I was going through, so I celebrated with and without people. I also realized that not everyone will want you to heal and move forward, and not everyone will support you. I now love to celebrate.

As you can see, my daughter, I view life as a reason to celebrate yourself. My life hasn't always been perfect, but I celebrated because it made me feel better, and allowed me to push past the pain. I also believe that, if you get into the habit of putting yourself first and celebrating yourself, it will make whatever situation you are dealing with less important than you. Celebrate you!

Cheers to you!

Dr. Carmesha Smith

Changing the Paradigm

Michaela R. Shaw

Superman is Black, and he is a woman.

Growing up, I came to understand the agreements society wrote for the Strong Black Woman. Her right to be a noun was taken away and she was defined as a verb—an action—born out of necessity, she did whatever needed to be done; rather, she became whatever the world needed. This ideology came complete with a cape, a community in trauma, an endless supply of forgiveness, an infinite stockpile of patience, a surplus of compassion, a godlike ability to make things work while maintaining an unbreakable exterior, and a near-perfect image and work ethic. These were the entry-level requirements for the position of Strong Black Woman I. To obtain level II, there were additional requirements such as the ability to carry a community, and the occasional ability to walk on water.

As a child, I watched my mother, grandmothers, great-grandmothers, and aunts (by blood and by community), feed those who were hungry, raise children without families, educate a community, and step in as birth workers and counselors to fill every crevice of potential need in order to smooth the path for those walking in their footsteps—for me. By thirteen years old, my home was at the intersection of excellence and advocacy. I was already a community doula and birth educator, a mentor, enrolled in college courses, an activist, and advocate; and on my way to becoming a Strong Black Woman (although I had yet to earn my cape). It is only now at seventeen, as I begin to step into womanhood, that I see the trauma, pain, and debilitating exhaustion that accompany these superhuman feats—the fear of failing others that sits just behind the wisdom, hugs, smiles, laughter, and love. When I sit in the space of a neutral observer, I am in awe of the women who have carried communities and cultures on their backs with apparent ease, undeniable poise, and flawlessness that only a Black woman can pull off; yet I am disheartened by their burden. Recently, I completed *The Four Agreements: A Practical Guide to Personal Freedom* by Don Miguel Ruiz. Upon reflection, I understand that the agreements these women live by are not their own, but rather the agreements that were placed by society or a failed agreement of another that needed to be completed for the "greater good." This saddens me.

The Black superwoman is often unseen; the last person we check on, yet the first we seek when we have a need. The ongoing cycle of pouring into others while holding an empty cup has to place these superheroes in a mental landscape of scarcity and selflessness that is detrimental. The burden that society has placed on the Strong Black Woman is another layer of abuse that extends and accompanies the generational trauma that has been passed from mother to daughter throughout the diaspora. I believe this trauma is embedded in our DNA and is viscerally within us. The mental health of the Strong Black Woman is at a breaking point; the collective is exhausted, drained, and in a constant state of post-traumatic stress and post-traumatic slave syndromes. It is time for my generation to take our place and help our mothers and grandmothers write their own agreements. I am grateful that my mother, the epitome of a Strong Black Woman, taught me to write my own contract (rather than inherit one), to breathe deeply, and to live the joy-led life I wish to lead. She taught me to serve while practicing self-care and maintaining my mental health. I hope that her generation is the last generation of Strong Black Women. As for me, she raised me to be a Free Black Woman—a woman who embodies strength and balance. Which Black woman are you going to be?

Afterword

I See You

Nykeia Maddrey

Black is beautiful

Queen stand and fix your crown

Your heart beats to the rhythm of a drum

So dance

For the battle was won by the tears that you cried caring for others

Celebrate

'Cause you told your story

Now walk through that finish line

Embracing every hiccup that made you pick up your pace

Smile

Let your light shine

For the darkness had to flee

'Cause you woke up and decided to write about the change that you saw in a vision far away but yet near

'Cause you dared to believe that you were the gift for this moment in time to birth a nation

To heal a people

And to unite cultures by speaking about love and by your unwavering actions

Rise beautiful Black woman

Take your rightful place

Where? You do say

In the front of the line

'Cause you waited so patiently

So productively

So in tune with the times that you provided your power as a resource

Because you were connected to THE source

Stand up and walk your victory lap

Because today we celebrate you

Beautiful Black woman, I see you

Our Authors

Aja K. Ellington - Founder & CEO, Free Your Wings Youth Mentoring, Inc.

Alicia R. Acklin - Empowered Woman

Alicia L. Littlejohn - Wife, Blogger, "Mother to Many"

Alicia Rodman - Certified Life Coach & Motivational Speaker

Allison T. Garrett - Certified Life Coach

Dr. Angee Valentine - Professor, CEO Platinum and Gold Presents, Author

Angel Morgan - Friend, Author & Blogger

Angelita Byrd - Entrepreneur, Mentor

www.AngelitaByrd.com

Annette Jackson - Transitional Life Coach, Author, Motivational Speaker

Dr. Ashley Valentine - Higher Education Professional, Autism Advocate

Dr. Aubria Nance - Educator, Student Success Advocate, Life Coach

www.NSCLeap.com

Brenda Searcy - Wife, Mother, Daughter, Sister, Friend

Britta Ofori-Kuragu, MSc - Purposeful Parenting Coach

Brunette Kirtdoll Smith - Mother, Grief and Mental Health Advocate

Cameasha Muhammad, M.A. - Transformation and Mindset Coach

Candia Cumberbatch-Lucenius - Owner, Healing and Comforting Hearts, LLC

Dr. Carmesha Smith - Mentor, Counselor, Professor, Mother, Sister

Carolyn Griffin - Mother, Grandmother, Sister, Friend

Cassandra Hill - Wellness Coach, Holistic Health Practitioner, Speaker

Dr. Charlotte Brickhouse - National Speaker, Wife, Mother, Spec Ed Advocate

Charlotte Miller-Lacy - Founder, I Am My Sister's Keeper

C Wilkinson Davis - Mental Health Advocate

Corinne M. Green - CEO, HR MOM LLC, Educator, Mother, Wife

www.HRMOMLLC.com

Dalila Zachary - Medical Doctor

Dana M. Harris - Mother, Sister, Friend

Danita L. Mosley - Serial Entrepreneur, Wife, Mother, Sister, Daughter

Darieth Chisolm - Emmy Award Winning TV Host, Speaker, Author

www.Darieth.com

Darla M. Character-Johnson, Esq. - Mother, Sister, Friend, Attorney

Dawn M. Perry - Creator, Navigation Series; Mother, Sister, Transformational Coach

Dee Outler - Peace & Conflict Resolution, LGBTQ Advocate, Mother

Deneen E. Mosley, M.Ed. - Owner, MECCA, LLC; Education Consultant

Diane Renee - Author, Publisher, Mother, Sister, Friend

Eli Thompson - Intuitive Lifestyle Transformation Coach, Public Speaker

Elon Jeffcoat - Artist

Emile Weatherspoon - Daughter, Sister, Friend

Essynce Moore - Essynce Couture LLC

www.EssynceCouture.com

Felicia Davis - Leadership Brand Strategist

F. Renee Hamilton - Attorney, Author

Frankie Roe - Author, Speaker, Career Coach

Gwen Buchanan - Health Coach

Heather D. Horton - Grief Recovery Coach, Lawyer

www.HeatherDHorton.com

India Thomas-Johns - Financial Advisor

Dr. Jacqueline Bingham Flemmings - Educator, Wife, Mother

Jamie Newton-Knight - Blended Family & Co-parenting Strategist

Jamillah Smith - Mentor, Diverse Leader, Lifelong Learner, Mother

Janell S. Foster, Juris Doctor - Grief Support Mentor, Wife, Mother

Janella Dobbs, MS, LPC, NCC - Psychotherapist

www.HLS4u.org

jSelene Thornton-Hubbard - Beauty for Ashes Ministry, Servant Leader, Psalmist

Janett V. Blanchard - Sister

Jeffonia P. Jones - Founder & CEO of The Strong Friend, LLC; Life Coach

Jeri Johnson, M.S. Ed., M.S. Sch Psy. - Educator, Daughter, Sister, Friend

Dr. Jessica A. Spradley - Educator, Mother, Daughter, Sister, Friend

Jinnell Killingsworth – Professor, Career Strategist

www.BlackCareerDiva.com

Kamela T. Smith, M.Ed. - An Unapologetically Unashamed Woman, Wife

Kathrine Henderson, LMSW - Wife, Mother, Sister, Friend

Keysha Bass - Business Coach

Kiana Romeo, MBA - Mother & Certified Life Breakthrough Coach

Kimberly H. Smith - Freelance Writer

Kurshay Whitaker - Daughter, Friend, College Student, Model

LaKichay Nadira Muhammad - Wholistic Health Practitioner, Therapist

www.TheCenterforSelfImprovement.com

Dr. LaShonda M. Jackson-Dean, DM, MBA, CPC - TV Network Owner, Author

Latasha Taylor - Makeup Artist

LaVerne Henderson - Licensed Hypnotist

Lisa Collins - Sacred Woman Practitioner

www.SoulAwakenGemz.com

Lisa Michelle Flynn - Wife, Mother, Daughter, Minister, Friend

Lois T. Miller, M.A. - Writer, Bible Teacher

Malaika Turner, Ph D. - Host of the Pivot Podcast, Speaker, Trainer

Malayah Rahman - Black Girl Magic

Malinda Bova - Author, Spiritual Goddess, Child Advocate

Dr. Marcia F. Robinson - The Workplace Evolutionist

Marcie Wilson - Professor, Minister, Teacher, Love Coach

Maria Josefina Fernandez - Personal Risk Account Manager, Visual Artist

Marilyn Pendelton, RN, M. Ed., LNC, CSN - Grief Recovery Method Specialist®

www.URVoiceHeard.org

Dr. Marla Wormley - Teacher, Sister, Friend

Marquita L. Allen - Health and Wellness Advocate, Coach

Mary Hazward Fernandez - Author, Speaker, Coach, CEO of W.O.H.I.

www.BusinessDevelopmentbyWOHI.com

Meagan Ferrare - Artiste

Melanie Townsend, MA, MSW - Mother, School Social Worker

Melissa Johnson Hewitt, MSW - Coach, Consultant, Confidant

Mia S. Bradford, MA - Financial Self-Care Coach; Beyond the Busyness

Michaela R. Shaw - Scholar, Artist, Advocate, Change Agent

Michelle A. Taylor - President & CEO, United Way of Delaware

Michelle Washington - Founder & CEO Women of More Creative Group

www.womenofmorecreativegroup.com

NaTasha Tierra - Agent of Change

Nathalie C. Lilavois, Ed.D. - Mother, Educator, Speaker, TEDx Curator

Nichole K. Sullivan - Mother

Nicole A. Johnson - Sister

Nicole Pettiway - Certified Health & Wealth Coach, Breast Cancer Thriver

Nicoli Rena Sinclair - Yoga and Meditation Instructor

Nisa K. Williams, M.Ed. MBA - Financial Literacy Coach

Noreen N. Henry - Victorious Living Strategist

www.NoreenNHenry.com

Nydia S. Wells-Evans - Transitional Speaker, DV Survivor/Advocate

www.NOLAPressure.com

Nykeia Maddrey - Mother, Friend, Spoken Word Poet

Petra Sherbin-Fox - Life Coach, Daughter, Mother, Sister, Friend

Quanisha M. Green, MSS - Founder/CEO, Black Woman CEO

www.BlackWomanCEO.com

R.A. Leigh Hawkins - Just a girl figuring it all out

Rachelle Byars-Sargent, M.A. PMC-III - Business Process Engineer

Rita Wells Gorder, M.A., - Lifestyle Consultant, Stylist, Career Coach

Roberta Oluwaseun Roberts, Esq. - Christian Lawyer Life Coach

Rochelle Peterson-Ansari - Consultant, Trainer & Coach

www.perceptionsunltd.com

Savannah Shepherd - Founder, DE Social Justice Remembrance Coalition

Shante R. Roddy - Talk Show Host, Business Development Trainer

www.SheBossTalk.com

Shirelle Diamond Hogans - International Empowerment Speaker

Stephanie Lewis - Professional Writer, Editor, Soldier of Peace

Tai Abrams, M.A. - Author, CEO, Money Mastery Coach

Tam Watkins - Firefighter/EMT, Life Coach Mentor and Speaker

Tanerra Willis - Author, Certified Pediatric Registered Nurse, Mentor

Tanisha L. Scott - Motivational Speaker, Life Coach

Taryn Washington - Ambassador, I Am My Sister's Keeper – Chester, PA

Tina C. Powers - Mom; President, I Am My Sister's Keeper – MD Chapter

Tina Natasha - Ambassador, I Am My Sister's Keeper – DE Chapter

Tonya L. Horn - Diversity, Inclusion & Equality Advocate

Dr. Torri Love Griffin, LPC - Transformational Love & Relationship Coach

Traci R. Green, MBA - Cancer Coach, Certified Aromatherapist

Trici Coleman - One of God's Best Ideas, Life Coach, Author

Trina Vessels - Minister, Educator, Owner, Certified Trichologist

Tynetta T. Brown - Defying the diagnosis, the rejection, the norm

Veronica Lynn Clark - Empowerment Coach

Yolanda Rahman - Mother, Wife, Living my best life

Dr. Zakia Y. Gates - Mother, Professor of Education

Our Sponsors

International Sponsors

www.PropelCon.com

www.IUMEWords.com

National Sponsors

MY BRANDING *Strategist*

www.MyBrandingStrategist.com

www.WomenWhoLaunchandLead.com

Power Circle Sponsors

www.WomenofMore.com

Darieth

www.Darieth.com

www.EssynceCouture.com

www.AfroseArt.com

Partners

Patrice Pullen, KW Advantage II

patricepullen.kw.com

I Am My Sisters' Keeper

www.IAmMSK.org

Works Cited

Cole, Keyshia and Curtis, Gregory G. *I Remember. On Just Like You [album].* Geffen (2007)

Degrasse Tyson, Neil. www.masterclass.com/classes/neil-degrasse-tyson-teaches-scientific-thinking-and-communication

Lomax, John A, Ruby T Lomax, and Doris McMurray. *This Little Light o' Mine.* Near Huntsville, Texas, 1939. Audio. Retrieved from the Library of Congress, www.loc.gov/item/lomaxbib000628/

Masser, M. and Creed, L. (Copyright 1977). The Greatest Love of All [Recorded by Whitney Houston]. On *Whitney Houston* [album]. Arista Records. (1983-1984)

Ruiz, Miguel, and Janet Mills. *The Four Agreements: A Practical Guide to Personal Freedom.*, 1997. Print.

Made in the USA
Coppell, TX
30 April 2021

54797908R00184